Also by Jon Katz

Rose in a Storm

Soul of a Dog

Izzy & Lenore

Dog Days

A Good Dog

Katz on Dogs

The Dogs of Bedlam Farm

The New Work of Dogs

A Dog Year

Geeks

Running to the Mountain

Virtuous Reality

Media Rants

Sign Off

Death by Station Wagon

The Family Stalker

The Last Housewife

The Fathers' Club

Death Row

Going
HOME

Going
HOME

Finding Peace When Pets Die

Jon Katz

VILLARD NEW YORK

Published in the United States by Villard,
an imprint of The Random House Publishing Group,
a division of Random House, Inc., New York.

RANDOM HOUSE and colophon are registered trademarks
of Random House, Inc.

ISBN 978-0-345-50269-8
eBook ISBN 978-0-345-52928-2

Printed in the United States of America

Random House website address: www.atrandom.com

2 4 6 8 9 7 5 3 1

First Edition

Photographs by Jon Katz
Book design by Susan Turner

Contents

CONTENTS

Introduction

It was my birthday, August 8, 2005. I had just brought Orson home from the vet's office, where he had been put down.

My other dog, Rose, who reads me better than any other living creature, froze when I got out of the truck. From her post on the hill with the sheep, she watched me take Orson's body out of the truck, her eyes never straying from the unwieldy package.

Rose herded the sheep over to their feeder, then turned, came quickly down to greet me, and sniffed Orson through the large plastic bag the vet had given me. She had spent every day of her life with Orson and was almost always around him. I wondered how she would react. She would smell his death, of course, and know it instantly.

As detached as a crime-scene investigator, she took note of the bag, and of Orson's smell. She gave the sheep a stern warning look over her shoulder and fell into place alongside me, as if she had expected this to happen. Nothing surprised Rose. I loved her for being so adaptable. It was as if she was telling me, "Hey, life goes on. Let's get this done and get back to work."

The late-afternoon clouds swept over the mountains and cast the hill in shadow. With Rose by my side, I made my way toward the top of the pasture where a handyman had dug a grave. Orson was the heaviest thing I have ever had to carry, in so many different ways. In that bag, along with the limp body of my dead dog, I carried a piece of my heart.

I had to stop two or three times—to put him down, catch my breath, swat the flies away, wipe my face with a handkerchief, gulp from the bottle of water in my back pocket. Each time, Rose waited for me. My back and legs hurt and I was in shock. Orson had died with his head in my lap, looking up at me, and I'd felt as if I might come apart. I didn't. I didn't want him to pick up on my fear or sadness at the end of his life, so I just smiled and said, "Thank you."

In 2000, a loving breeder in Texas told me she was seeking a home for a border collie who had failed to make it as a show dog. He was intense but intelligent, she said. He was beautiful. He had issues. I brought him into my life for reasons that are still not clear to me.

Orson did not turn out to be an ordinary dog in any respect. He crashed into my life like a meteor, and was so charismatic, rebellious, and explosive a personality that I abandoned my life as a mystery writer and media critic, began taking sheepherding lessons, bought Bedlam Farm, and ended up with a menagerie: donkeys, sheep, steers, and, for a while, some goats. I loved Orson dearly, although he drove me crazy from the moment I first picked him up at Newark Airport. Animal lovers know that troubled creatures are sometimes the ones we love most.

On the farm, Orson wreaked havoc, which was his dominant characteristic. He dug under and leapt over fences. His notion of sheepherding was to grab the largest ewe and pull her over onto the ground. He was intensely arousable. And, unfortunately, overprotective. Orson nipped at workmen, package-delivery people, neighbors. He bit three people, including a child. My beloved dog defied treatment from the best and most expensive veterinarians, holistic practitioners, trainers, and animal communicators. He was simply beyond my ability to repair or control.

Still, Orson taught me a lot about my own limits, and he also sparked a process that made me not just a writer but a writer about dogs, farms, and rural living. He was the dog who changed my life.

One of the many gifts Orson led me to was Rose, another border collie. Working with Orson, I came to love border collies and was mesmerized by the rituals and practices of herding sheep with them.

I got Rose when she was just eight weeks old. A small, beautiful, black-and-white creature, she was, from the first, my partner on the farm, helping me with herding and lambing. She battled coyotes and pigs, fought off rabid feral cats and skunks, and twice saved my life. Each time, I had fallen on the ice during an awful winter storm and knocked myself out. I would have frozen to death in the bitter cold if Rose had not awakened me by nipping on my ears.

Like Orson, Rose has had a profound impact on my life, making it possible, in many ways, for me to live on a farm. She and Orson were as inseparable as they were different.

Orson gave me so much, and I repaid him by ending his life. He was troubled, damaged, and I spent years trying to fix him, to no avail. I talked to my vet and we agreed that he should be euthanized. There was nothing left to try, no more money to spend. It was an agonizing decision, but I had to trust that it was the right one.

It took me a while to get Orson up the hill that day. Rose no longer paid overt attention to the bag, yet I could tell she was aware of it. She was always with me when there was work to do, pleasant or not.

The grave site at the top of the pasture was a beautiful

spot, with a commanding view of the farm and the hills and valley beyond.

Orson would love it up there, I hoped. I dug the hole deeper to prevent predators from getting into the grave. Sweat soaked my clothes now, and the flies feasted on my arms and face. Ever vigilant, Rose sat nearby watching me and keeping an eye on the sheep below.

After I buried Orson carefully, I placed the marker, a flat slab of stone carved with his name, at the head of his grave. I shook my head. I wanted to cry but could not, though the pain I felt was piercing.

I had lost dogs before, but not this dog, and not in this way. This one really hurt.

I was awash in guilt, grief, and loss. And I was alone. I didn't know how to deal with the pain I was feeling, or how to mourn this dog, whom I loved beyond words and owed so much. He had been such an integral part of my life—not only had he inspired me to change my life for the better, but he had lived each of those changes with me. We had traveled all over the country together—on book tours, to herding trials, even to the University of Minnesota, where I taught for a few months.

But even so, I was embarrassed by my grief. Perhaps that shame was due to my gender and a long-held tendency to hide emotions and bury feelings. I didn't feel like calling up my friends or the people I worked with to tell them I was in mourning over a dog. What would they think of me? Human beings died every day in the world, and suffered illness, catastrophes, and great misfortune. What right did I have to fall to pieces over a border collie? I heard my father's voice clearly: *Suck it up.*

I did not want to be one of those silly people who lost themselves in the lives of their dogs and cats. I didn't want people to see how I felt. I told myself that Orson was just a dog, an animal. It wasn't like he was human. Yet my grief could hardly have been worse. I admitted to myself that I had lost members of my family for whom I had not felt that much sorrow. It was a shocking thing to concede.

But the truth is that my relationship with Orson was simpler, more productive, and even more loving than many of the relationships within my human family. Losing a border collie is not like losing a parent, yet I felt closer to this crazy dog than I ever felt to my own father. And I hear this so often from other dog owners as well. How does one make sense of that?

Grief doesn't always come with perspective. It doesn't differentiate between the things we feel and the things we ought to feel. The love of a dog can be a powerful thing, in part, I think, because animals are a blank canvas upon which we can—and do—paint almost anything. Dogs enter our lives and imprint themselves in ways that people, and our complex relationships with them, cannot.

Maybe it would have been easier if I'd had his body cremated. Briefly, I regretted my choice. Cremation seemed simpler, more private. The process would have been more indirect and somehow neater. His body would be gone, returned to me as ashes that I could scatter in the woods or up on the hill. I told myself that there wouldn't have been as much mourning required, but I knew that wasn't the case.

I poured more dirt onto his grave and then tamped down the earth with heavy rocks to keep it secure. I closed my eyes, felt the cooling evening breeze slide up the hill, and offered a moment of silence. Rose watched me until I was done and then went down the hill and back to the sheep, who had drifted somewhere she didn't want them to go for reasons I would never know.

When I came down the hill, I was determined not to tell anyone how I felt. I didn't want to appear sentimental or, God forbid, weak. I wanted to move on. I wanted to keep perspective. I went to work. But all I could think about was Orson. I couldn't focus. I had to talk to someone.

I called my daughter and told her Orson was dead.

"I'm so sorry," she said. "How are you?"

"Okay," I answered.

"It must have been hard," she said.

"No," I told her quickly. "Not really. I made the right decision. I'm comfortable with it."

And I wasn't completely off. In a sense, I *was* comfortable with my decision. It was a good decision, well considered and thought through. Orson had bitten people, and I couldn't be sure he wouldn't do it again. I had spent many thousands of dollars on dog trainers, psychics, pills, shamans, holistic practitioners, veterinary druggists, and acupuncture. I even ordered him some calming medicine from China. Perhaps I ought to have taken it myself. There wasn't anything else I could do for Orson.

Though I believed I had made the right decision, I had no notion of how to process my grief. I didn't know how to say goodbye, how to mourn the things I lost. I didn't know how to show that pain to other human beings—an essential element of healthy grieving.

I resisted telling the people I loved how much I hurt, how much I mourned for this troubled dog. There is a community of grief where countless millions have been, dwell, or will go. When it comes to animals, that community is vast; its shared sense of pain and loss is palpable and deep. But what is it that makes the community more than something intangible, more than an idea or a notion? How do we find it? Join it? Make it real?

I think we can become a part of this healing community by acknowledging grief and loss and pain. By asking for help. By opening up. By coming to consciousness, permitting the loss and welcoming grief, revealing it, respecting it. By understanding the loss without succumbing to it.

By not allowing myself to grieve Orson and discuss my loss, I skated over the experience and failed to see its significance. The death of Orson was a watershed moment in my life. It deserved attention and respect. My reaction to his death said much about me: how closed off I was, how vulnerable, how little I really grasped of my own life. I was afraid of my grief and wouldn't allow myself to see why his death mattered so much.

I see it better now. Orson entered my life at a time of great need. And though he had his problems, he also led me out of a place I did not want to be and guided me to a new chapter in my life. He brought me to my farm. He brought me to a life that I loved, and a person with whom I loved sharing it. He taught me limits and boundaries. He gave me perspective. He forced me to learn how to respect myself and my own decisions—a great gift. All this I came to see in time.

Perhaps it is time for this particular form of grief to come out of the closet and into the open. The loss of a beloved pet can be painful, even devastating. Mourning isn't comfortable, but it's a natural part of the grieving process and helps one move on.

No one is foolish for grieving for a dog or cat. A pet is rarely "just a dog" or "just a cat"; he is often an integral part of one's life, providing a loving emotional connection that has great meaning in a complex and cruel world.

I decided to write this book, sad reader—and if you're reading this, you probably *are* sad—because I thought it might be helpful.

I want to help animal lovers grieve when their pain is great.

And find perspective when it is hard to come by.

And celebrate the lives of their dogs and cats as well as mourn them.

And then move on.

My wish in writing this book is, in part, to convey the idea that the loss of a beloved dog or cat or horse does not have to be the end of something. It can be the beginning, a process as well as a loss. It is a gateway to the next experience.

Aristotle wrote that to truly know how to love something, you have to lose something. In that way, every animal I have lost has been a gift.

I want to pass along what I have learned.

I hope it helps.

Going
HOME

Animal Dreams
ORSON

In my dreams, dogs don't die.
In my dreams, my dogs talk to me.
They speak to me of life and loss, of love and joy, of the gates through which they entered and left my life. This is comforting. And nourishing. And very real to me. My dogs touch me in ways that stick. And that does not die.

ORSON

Orson emerges from a sea of bright blue lights, ranging
up a verdant hillside under misty skies.
Will you talk with me? I ask.
Of course, he says.
Will you forgive me? I plead.
For what? he asks.
For not being better.
For not fixing you.
For letting you die.
The lights all flicker in the gentlest of breezes.
His bright eyes meet mine.
You didn't kill me, he says.
*It was my time to go. It was my way of leaving,
of saying goodbye, of going home.*
Where did you go?
I came here, to rest, and to wait.
*And I came back to see you. I put my head on your foot
while you worked, and watched over you. You seemed sad,
alone.*
*Then you saw why I brought you to the farm,
why I came into your life, and led you to a different place.*
So you could find work you loved.
And find yourself.
And find someone to love.
You did that?
He is silent, staring beyond me.

*We come and we go, entering the lives of people
at different points, in different ways. When we are called, we
leave. It doesn't really matter how we go; there are many
ways for us to leave. I wish I could have told you that you
didn't have that much power over us, to decide our fates.
I was ready to move on, and so were you. Ready to find
another kind of love. To change your work. To find out who
you are. I could only do so much. You had to do the rest.*
Did you love me?
*Yes, always. But not in your way. Not only you. We serve
human beings, and we love them all. In our own way, we
protect and guide, and fill some of the holes in your lives.*
And then he touched his nose to my hand, and he moved
off, disappearing into the lights.
I will always be close by, he says.

The
Good Life

THERE IS SOMETHING ELEMENTAL, even beautiful, about the natural death of an animal. When a pet dies naturally, it frees us from the agonizing second-guessing and guilt that can accompany the decision to euthanize it in order to spare it suffering. Still, the experience of having a pet die naturally has its own pain, as well as its own opportunities for gratitude and love.

Julia, a nurse in Kansas City, wrote me about her dog Spike, a fourteen-year-old mixed breed adopted from a shelter when he was a puppy. Spike suffered from arthritis and had some colon and kidney problems. He was on a special diet. Julia knew he was getting old, but he was still eating, still able to walk outside and follow her around the house. During his last exam, the vet had said that his heart was weakening. She warned Julia that Spike could go at any time.

Julia talked to the vet about how Spike might die, and the vet said that since the dog's health problems weren't particularly severe or painful, he might well die naturally. This was difficult to hear, but Julia was relieved that the vet wasn't recommending toxic drugs or scary procedures. She didn't want to put Spike through that.

One night, as she sat reading a novel, Spike climbed up onto the sofa and put his head in her lap. Julia remembered enjoying the pleasure of a good book and the fire crackling in front of them when something made her look up. She sensed, rather than saw or heard, a change. "Suddenly, Spike wasn't breathing. He was gone. I knew it."

She was surprised by how calm she felt. Instead of being upset, she felt full of love for her dear friend. She sat with him for a while, then picked him up and laid him on his bed. In the morning she took him to the vet's office for cremation. The ashes are now in a small urn on the fireplace mantel.

"How lucky I was to have him go that peacefully, and with me. I felt tremendous grief, but I didn't have to make the decision about his life that I had always dreaded making. And he didn't die with stitches all over or tubes in his nose, or drugged. He had always had a good life. And he died a good way. Recognizing that made me feel a whole lot better."

I love the idea of the Good Life. I believe this notion can be an enormous help to people who have lost their pets. The fact that Spike had had a good life was a great comfort to Julia. It gave her perspective; something to take pride in. When you clear away all of the emotional confusion, there is this: all we can give our pets is a Good Life. We can't do more than that. We miss them because that life was good, loving, and joyful. Too often this truth is lost in our grieving.

When I was a teenager I joined a Quaker meeting. I loved many things about the Quakers but was especially drawn to their notion of death. When someone or something dies, rather than mourn, the Quakers celebrate the life. They laugh and sing and tell funny stories about the person who is gone, and they remember the very best things about that person's life. What a lesson for those of us who have lost a dog or a cat who has meant a lot to us. And that is just what Julia did for Spike. She didn't just mourn the dog she lost, she celebrated the life they had together. The Good Life.

Over the years I've heard many wonderful stories about dogs who die a natural death, who say goodbye in their own way and time. Donna told me about her Welsh corgi, Cora, who went off into the garden for her final sleep one summer afternoon and was found lying in a bed of hostas, at peace. Raiki, an elderly golden retriever who lived in northeastern Vermont, was struggling to walk, eat, and see. One winter's night she walked off into a blizzard and was never found. Jen and Peter, who loved her, believe that she became a spirit of the wind, and that she blows back to them with each storm.

Dan, an Upstate New York logger, would let Sadie, his ferocious rottweiler/shepherd out of his truck at 5 A.M. every day, and she would return faithfully about twelve hours later when his work was done. He never knew where she went or what she did, but she often came back limping, bleeding, covered in scratch and claw marks. Sadie was aging and was now stiff with joint pain. One morning, after she scrambled out of the truck, she paused and stared into his eyes for the longest time. He had ridden with this wild and beautiful creature for ten years, but he had never seen her look at him in this way. When she finally limped off, he knew that he would never see her again. And he didn't.

"I was happy for her," he said. "She died the way she wanted to die."

She had, he said, a Good Life.

To give a creature a Good Life is a precious thing.

As your pet ages and you sense the end may be near, focus your mind on the best parts of the life you shared. On love. Loyalty. Comfort. Laughter. Remember that you still have time. Record your memories. You might want to take some photos or make a video. Consider gathering friends to say goodbye. And lift your heart in celebration of the amazing gift of loving an animal's spirit—and being loved in return.

Finally, it might help ease your sadness to ask yourself the following questions:

Did I give my pet the best life I could?
Did I feed him every single day of his life?
Did I care for him when he was sick?
Did I take him with me whenever I could?
Did I appreciate and return his affection?
Did I recognize and honor his true nature?
Did I love him?
Do I miss him?
Did he have a Good Life?

If the answer to these questions is yes, know and re-member that you gave a special animal a Good Life.

Speaking for Your Pet

WHEN YOU BRING A DOG INTO YOUR home, some powerful realities come along with him.

Most likely, he will not outlive you. Nor will he be able to tell you his wishes for the future or the precise nature of his suffering.

Your dog may die naturally of old

age, but it is more probable that you will have to decide when it is time for him to die.

Many of us—almost all of us perhaps—believe at one time or another that our dogs think the way we do, and even that we know what they're thinking. Humans are both emotional and presumptuous by nature; we feel that if we love something, it must be like us.

We are inclined to project our own thoughts and emotions into the minds of our pets, especially at the end of their lives when there are painful and agonizing decisions to be made and our own emotions are churning.

Some people say that their pets will tell them when it's time to go. I don't believe that. No animal of mine has ever told me he was ready to die. I wish it were that simple. Dogs can communicate but they cannot talk, nor do they think in our language or on our terms. There is no evidence that an animal can take on the sophisticated task of deciding to end his life and to communicate that decision to us.

I believe in advocacy. Advocacy for animals can mean a lot of things. Animal rescue. Animal rights. Ethical breeding. No-kill shelters. Loving care. It also means taking responsibility for dogs when they most need us, and our dogs never need us more than at the end of their lives. The most critical moment in my relationship with a dog—and the toughest—is the time when I must become his or her advocate. One of the most complex decisions those of us who love animals will ever make—the one that causes the most pain, guilt, grief, and regret—is when to let go.

Taking responsibility and having faith in your own judgment will help you make good choices and decisions at the end of your pet's life. The words of the great moral philosophers, more than anything else, have helped and guided me in these decisions. Their tenets and ideas have given me the strength and confidence to make my own good choices, and to trust in those choices so that what I felt for my dying animals was grief and loss separate from guilt, self-loathing, and regret.

If you read Plato, Thomas Aquinas, Hannah Arendt, and the other great scholars of animal responsibility, you find some common threads and universal values. They can help build a foundation of what I call tolerable and appropriate grief. Grief that is natural, even healing.

Philosophers note that humans and animals differ in lots of ways. One of the most elemental differences is that we can make moral choices. We have consciences. We can discern right and wrong. We know we will die. We are afraid of pain and loss.

Animals do none of these things.

They are instinctive creatures who live in the moment. They experience emotions and pain but are not aware of them as concepts to think about and ponder. They die but don't know they will die. Animals read our emotions but not our minds. They might know that we are upset or anxious but not that we are upset or anxious about them or their impending death.

This is where responsibility and judgment come in. Because we can make these decisions, we are responsible. Let go of the idea that you and your dog can make a joint decision, or that he can make it for you. You must be the one to decide—please don't let yourself off the hook.

When Orson, a dog to whom I owed—and continue to owe—so much, bit a child and drew blood from his arm and then bit a young gardener in the neck, a boundary was crossed. His contract with the world was broken in a way that could not be repaired. I will never forget the sight of that blood.

I could have confined him, sent this hyperactive border collie into a prison for the rest of his life. I could have abdicated my responsibility and given him to someone else. I could have ignored his potential to harm people.

Instead, I chose to speak for him. To be his advocate as well as an advocate for other people, other children. I had to decide whether I valued human life and safety over a dog I loved.

I resolved that I would never again be responsible for the flow of human blood. Once Orson had bitten first one person, then a second, then a third, I could never again say that I did not know it might happen. I felt that the only humane way I could be sure that he would never attack another human was to euthanize him.

We need to speak for our dogs because they cannot speak to us. Because they do not understand illness and death beyond their own extraordinary instincts. Because they do not have language or narrative. Because they are not, as far as we know, conscious of their choices or even that there is a choice to be made.

As advocates, we literally become our dogs' voices, their representatives and guardians. It is how we honor that unspoken but powerful contract that has connected us to dogs for thousands of years. We owe it to them.

Speaking clearly and compassionately for the animals we love is perhaps the most important foundation for grieving that is natural, healthy, and as free as possible of doubt and guilt. Advocating for your pet is what will allow you to move on. Speak for him. Speak for yourself. Be loving and gentle to both.

Over the years I've gotten countless letters from vets and vet techs describing what happens when humans can't let go. These letters are full of sad stories about dogs and cats suffering, gasping for breath, struggling with pain, swathed in bandages and stitches, confused and fearful, for days, even months.

Here, loving readers, is what I think about that.

We have to let go. Hanging on is not love. Dogs and cats did not come into our lives to suffer, or to stay beyond their time because of our wants and needs.

Look for that sign that lets you know "it's time." Be brave. You can see it if you look. That calm, reasonable voice inside yourself will tell you, if you listen. Or simply ask your vet; be open to that painful but necessary conversation.

So:
Listen to the animals.
What feelings do they communicate?
Do they suffer?
Has the light gone out?
Is the spirit lost?

When the cost is too great.
When they struggle for life.
If they cannot live their lives.
If keeping them alive is for you and not them.
Then, please.
Show true love.
Do what is merciful.
Learn what it means to be selfless,
to know gratitude.
Speak for them,
when they cannot speak

for themselves.
When you know
it is time for them to go.

Listen to them.
And let go.

The
Perfect Day

I BELIEVE IT IS POSSIBLE TO TAKE something beautiful and lasting out of the heart-wrenching experience of seeing the animal you love move inexorably toward the end of life. Nobody can take the grief away, nor should anyone try, but our love for animals is nothing but a gift, and it keeps on giving, even when they go home.

A man named Harry, an Iraq War veteran and tennis coach from Minnesota, hit upon a simple and profound idea to transform this otherwise sad experience into a blessed one.

It was a gray morning when the vet told Harry that his dog Duke's heart was failing and that it wouldn't be long before he died. Harry was not surprised, but still, the news depressed him. Listening to the vet, Harry later told me, he'd gotten an idea, one he thought would pay tribute to his life with Duke and give him something to feel besides sadness and loss.

"Tomorrow, I'm going to give you a Perfect Day," he said quietly to Duke as they left the vet's office. He would take the day off from work and create a sweet memory with his dog. It would be a special day, filled with all the things Duke loved most, as close to perfect as Harry could make it. He would take his Canon PowerShot along to capture some images of the day, to preserve the memories.

Duke was a border collie/shepherd mix. He had always been a lively, energetic dog and would herd anything that moved. Walks, work, food, Frisbees, red balls—these were the things Duke loved, along with chasing balloons and popping them.

Harry went shopping for supplies, and when he came back Duke was napping on his dog bed. He went over, lay down next to the dog, and hugged him. "Pal," he whispered, "tomorrow is for you, your Perfect Day." He was embarrassed to tell his wife, Debbie, about the plan, but she sensed what was going on and gave the two of them the space they needed. It was her belief that the dog, more than anything else, helped Harry heal from the trauma of Iraq. He couldn't look at Duke without smiling, and when he had first come home, he hadn't smiled too often.

At eight the next morning, Harry got up. Duke was lying on his bed, which was next to Harry and Debbie's. The dog rose a bit slowly, then followed Harry down the stairs and into the kitchen. Harry opened the refrigerator and took out a hamburger patty and two strips of bacon, cooked the night before. He put them on a plate and into the microwave.

Duke was riveted. When the plate came out—Harry touched it to make sure it was warm but not hot—he dumped the meat into Duke's bowl, along with his heart pills. It was as if Duke couldn't believe his eyes. He was almost never given people food. Looking up at Harry, as if asking permission, he waited until Harry nodded and said, "Okay, boy," before inhaling the food.

A feeling of sadness came over Harry as he thought about how Duke would soon be gone. He wandered into the living room and lay down on the couch. Duke came over and curled up next to him. Harry began to sob, softly, then more deeply and loudly; Duke gently licked his face.

After a few minutes, Harry rose to get dressed. Although he worried about straining the dog's heart, he let Duke follow him up the stairs. On this day, Duke could do anything he wanted. No corrections. He sat on the bedroom floor and watched Harry put his clothes on. When Harry said "Sneakers," Duke labored to get up onto his feet, walked over to the closet, and brought Harry his white running shoes. Harry had enjoyed training his dog to bring him his sneakers, and Duke seemed to love it too.

Harry went back downstairs, followed by Duke. He picked up a bag from the pantry and walked out into the yard. Inside the bag were two dozen high-bounce red balls. One at a time, he threw them and bounced them off the back fence. Duke tore after one gleefully, then another, catching some, narrowly missing others as they whizzed past his head.

When Duke started to pant, Harry stopped.

Next they went to the town pond. Harry sat by the water's edge while Duke waded in, paddled around, swam back, shook himself off, then repeated the routine about a dozen times. Every few minutes Harry tossed the dog a liver treat. It practically rained the small and pungent treats. Once again, Duke looked as if he could hardly believe his good fortune.

They came back to the house and napped. After lunch, Harry took Duke to the vast state park outside of town. He picked a flat, gentle trail, and the two of them walked a couple of miles. Eventually, they came to a stone abutment with a beautiful view. Harry walked over to the edge and sat down. Duke clambered out and curled up beside him. It was a gorgeous afternoon, and the wind ruffled the dog's hair. Duke held his nose up to the wind, picking up the scents of the earth.

God, I love this creature, Harry thought. I never feel this peaceful, this much at ease. It is something to remember, to honor.

They sat together for nearly an hour, enjoying a bond of complete understanding and affection. If only the world could stay like this, Harry thought, this simple, this good.

Harry knew that Duke was tired, so they took their time walking back, stopping frequently to rest. A few years earlier, Duke could have hiked all day, and sometimes they did that together. But not anymore.

When they got home, Harry cooked Duke some prime sirloin, then chopped it up. The dog was beside himself, looking up at Harry as he ate, expecting the food to be taken away. That evening, Harry put one of his favorite Clint Eastwood movies into the DVD player and Duke hopped up onto the couch, put his head in Harry's lap, and went to sleep. When the movie was over, Harry carried the dog up the stairs and laid him down on his bed.

Several weeks after the Perfect Day, when Harry came home from work, Duke was not there by the door to greet him, and he knew he was gone. He went into the living room to find Duke dead. He knelt by his dog, closed his eyes, and said a prayer. Then he dug a deep hole in the backyard and buried Duke there, along with some bones, his collar, and some of his beloved red balls.

Of all the photos Harry took on the Perfect Day, the one he loved the best was of Duke sitting out on the stone ledge in the state park, taking in the sights and smells. Now every morning before he goes to work, he flips open his cellphone and smiles at the picture of Duke, looking for all the world like a king surveying his territory.

Harry passed on the idea of the Perfect Day to friends and other dog owners struggling to come to terms with their own pets' failing health. Many have since shared with him the stories of their dog's Perfect Day. It makes him happy to think about Duke's legacy—all those Perfect Days for all those other great dogs leaving our world behind.

Making a Decision You Can Live With

EVERYONE HAS TO MAKE THEIR OWN decisions, but I do not believe dogs were put on the earth to suffer, or to live impaired lives in which they cannot function as dogs—moving freely, eliminating outside, and being free of pain.

When my Lab Stanley was stricken

with heart disease, he could barely walk to his food bowl, could no longer take a single step toward his beloved red and blue rubber balls, and gasped for almost every breath. I saw that he could no longer live the life of a healthy dog and decided as his advocate that he needed to leave me and the world behind.

Stanley had come into my life shortly after I left the corporate media world—CBS News—to become a writer. I went to a breeder in northern New Jersey and got two sweet yellow Labs, Julius and Stanley. I had no clue how much they would change my life. Like all good working dogs, these two were looking for a job, and they found one as my writing dogs.

Julius and Stanley were the two mellowest dogs I have ever owned. They disliked frantic activity and were frightened of big waves. My kind of dogs. They loved to sit by the computer, accompany me on my long, brooding walks, and delight the children of the neighborhood. They were both wonderful ambassadors for dogs. Each opened my eyes to the ways in which dogs mark particular periods of life and shape them.

I've learned that dogs come and go, for their own reasons, at their own time. I am more accepting of that now, although I was not when these two loving creatures were stricken within months of each another. Julius was diagnosed with cancer, Stanley with heart disease. Julius's cancer progressed rapidly and savagely, and he declined quickly. There were no decisions to make. He died on the floor of our vet's office.

Stanley's illness was slower, more complex. When he developed congestive heart failure, I knew I had to make a decision. His death would spare him—and me—further suffering and expense. It was his time.

The decision to let an animal die, or to euthanize one, is as profoundly moral a decision as it is personal and difficult. You must deal not only with your loss but also with your uncertainty that you are making the right choice. That uncertainty can prolong grief.

Did you make the right decision? Can you move on?

Honestly, nobody can answer these questions but you.

Try to take solace in your decision. Trust that you made the right one.

Here are some things that might help you do that:

Consider the Welfare of the Animal

Is she in pain? What is her quality of life? Can she live the life of a normal dog? Is she in danger? Is she endangering other people or dogs?

Think About Your Feelings and Those of Other People

What will the impact of the animal's death be on you? Your family? The other people who depend on that animal for companionship, affection, and a connection to the world? Are you thinking of yourself and other people or of the needs of your pet? The animal comes first. Then us.

Gather All the Information You Can

Read whatever relevant books you can find, and go online to research a disease or surgery, if that's appropriate. Talk to your family and friends. Consult a breeder, rescue group, or vet.

I like vets. They are knowledgeable, compassionate, and supportive. Many vets say they are uncomfortable raising the idea of euthanasia because they feel it should come from their clients, not from them. If my pet is suffering, I always ask, "Should we consider euthanasia? Is it time? Will you tell me when it is?" Vets, like our own doctors, often offer only the options that will keep the animal alive, because it's what they're trained to do. But if you give them the opportunity, most will talk frankly about euthanasia, if they feel it's time. Ask your vet.

Breeders, veteran shelter workers, and rescue volunteers also know animals well and can be helpful resources. If you're worried or confused, call them, or email them, or go see them.

There are lots of people to talk to during this process, but be prepared: people give advice freely and will be only too happy to tell you what to do. While it is useful to gather information and opinions, remember that in the end this is your decision, not theirs.

Consider Cost

Many people find themselves in a vet's office making expensive decisions about surgery or medication because they feel they have to prove their love for a dog. A friend told me that she had spent twenty thousand dollars on a number of surgeries for her pug with liver problems.

"Is there any limit?" I asked her.

"No, none," she said. "That's how much I love my dog."

I told her I disagreed. If you believe your love for your pet is measured in money, you will end up spending a lot. To me, this is love misplaced, not proven. I would not subject any of my dogs to multiple surgeries, nor can I afford to spend twenty thousand dollars on them. I believe that it's not ethical or appropriate in this world to spend that kind of money on a dog while so many human beings suffer so much. But those are the beliefs that spur my own decisions, not hers. My friend wasn't wrong for spending twenty thousand dollars on her dog's health—it was her money and her choice—but spending money on surgeries isn't always what is best for the animal.

It's difficult for us to maintain perspective when it comes to our pets. It is critical that we—and our families—think about how much money we are comfortable spending to prolong an animal's life and make this decision in advance.

How far do you want to go? How much money do

you want to spend? How long do you all wish to prolong an animal's life? It's okay to spend thousands of dollars (to sell the big-screen TV to pay for the surgery). It's okay to say no, I can't afford that. Or to conclude that human priorities come first. Or to avoid debt and financial stress. It's not for me to say what's best for you and your pet.

Whatever you decide, don't leave it till the last minute. People who have not thought these issues through *before* their animal is suffering might find themselves in a vet's office having to make instant and expensive decisions about complex medical procedures.

If you can set limits before the final days, when you are overwhelmed with emotion, the decisions you have to make might be a lot easier. Think of the people who sign living wills so their families will not have to make agonizing decisions about prolonging their lives. Do the same for your dog or cat.

Nobody who gets a new pet wants to give a second's thought to its death. But if you can think about it somewhere along the way, you will be grateful later.

Decision Time

Nobody knows your dog or cat like you do. Nobody has the right to tell you what to do. Animal politics in America are just as noxious as the kind you see on cable news channels. People have strong opinions, and many seem to think they know more about your animal's welfare than you do. This is not true.

You have lived with this dog, loved her, fed her, cleaned up her messes, and trained her (hopefully). You can read her signals better than any outsider can.

I offer you the wisdom of Hannah Arendt, who spent a brilliant lifetime studying moral decision making. I find myself turning to her wonderful book *Responsibility and Judgment* again and again. "Moral conduct," she wrote, "seems to depend primarily on the intercourse of man with himself."

We must not contradict ourselves by making exceptions in our own favor. We must not place ourselves in a position where we despise ourselves. This enables us not only to *tell* right from wrong but also to *do* right.

Look inward to the best source of information there is: you. Then, when you have made your decision, look in the mirror. Say it out loud. If you respect yourself, then you have made the right choice.

Feel Confident About Your Decision

Tell yourself that you did the best you could do, based on the best information you could get. You were responsible. You used your best judgment.

Do not look back, agonize about it, or second-guess yourself.

Focus instead on the many things you gave your pet and the many things he or she gave you. The walks. The affection. The connections to other people. The shared experience of journeying through parts of life together.

That, not guilt or regret, is the legacy of your pet.

Animals cannot talk to us, but I imagine that if they could, they would say something like this:

"Speak for me. Help me to make the decisions that I cannot make. Do not ask me to tell you when it's time for me to go, for that is beyond my simple province. I love you and trust you, and I have depended on you all of my life to make decisions for me. Now, when I need you the most, do not fail me. Whatever you decide, I know it will be your best decision, and I wish you nothing but peace with it."

Responsibility
and Judgment

DECIDING TO SHORTEN OR END THE
life of a being you love dearly is one of
the most difficult choices you will ever
make. There are few tenets to follow
or guideposts to direct us. We must go
our own way, on our own path. Often,
great pain and loss are involved. And

sometimes lots of money. Other people's opinions. Our own myriad insecurities.

We feel responsible. We question our judgment. We seek approval. We feel guilty. If we're not careful, these all-too-human anxieties can blind us to the needs of the animals who depend on us.

I have had to make many decisions to end the lives of animals—dogs, cats, sheep, rabid raccoons, and skunks. Deciding to euthanize Orson was perhaps the hardest, but living on a farm, I have learned that when you live with animals, you must also live with their deaths.

I adopted Elvis, a three-thousand-pound Swiss steer, to spare him from the slaughterhouse. The crusty old farmer who brought him to me said that he was the first steer in forty years he couldn't bear to put on the truck to market. "He just follows me around like a puppy," he said. "I've never seen a steer do that."

The farmer was correct. Elvis was an affable monster. He loved people. And he loved me, especially after I started bringing him apples and carrots. I read him poems and stories in the pasture, fed him chocolate donuts and bananas. Elvis had the smart dog's gift of paying attention to people and making us believe that he loved us dearly. Maybe he did. That's why he had avoided a trip to the slaughterhouse and gotten such good care.

Elvis arrived at a turning point in my life. I was heading toward a divorce and mired in a savage bout of depression and anxiety. I was ready to love something. That something was Elvis.

It was, from the first, complicated. And I was unprepared.

For starters, I had to buy a tractor so I could move the big round bales of hay he ate, not to mention the enormous amounts of manure. I had to bring water to the far pasture and fend off the rats that came to eat the grain he needed. I had to spray him with insecticide to keep the monstrous flies away.

At first it was worth it. I loved Elvis. He was great company and a photographer's dream. People thought he was cute and loved the photos of him posted on my blog.

But over time I started to feel uneasy about him, especially as I began to confront other issues in my life—anxiety, reckless spending, competing impulses, and a need to make the farm dramatic and challenging. For a long time I had gotten whatever I wanted and given little thought to the cost. Now I was coming to terms with my life and beginning to take responsibility for it. I was growing up, at last, and painfully. I couldn't afford Elvis and all of the things that were needed to care for him.

Adopting Elvis was an act of love, but as I slogged through the devastating aftermath of a broken marriage—all of the emotional and financial consequences—I realized that it was also an act of delusion and immaturity. I simply couldn't keep him.

But you don't send Swiss steers to retirement homes or assisted-living facilities, and no sane farmer would dream of having one for a pet. Elvis was beginning to have leg troubles, and if they got any worse, I would have no choice but to have him shot right on the farm. Very few steers die of old age, and their health problems are expensive and either difficult or impossible to treat. There aren't many ways to get these big and powerful animals to hold still for treatment or take their pills.

Killing Elvis was not the ending I wanted. He was not in terrible pain, but I couldn't see any other options. Taking responsibility meant making sure that his death would be as humane as possible.

I visited the three renderers in the area, and I asked them—and saw—how they killed animals like Elvis.

It was not pretty. It did not make my decision easier. But there was one facility in central Vermont that used sedatives so that the animals did not feel pain. The owner promised that Elvis wouldn't be standing around for hours and that his end would be quick. I called a farmer I knew and told him that if he would take Elvis to be slaughtered, we could split the money. He was struggling to keep his farm afloat and eagerly agreed. I planned to donate my half of the proceeds to a local homeless shelter desperate for funds to feed the people who lived there.

The farmer came by one Saturday with a friend and a trailer. He put up a fence to corral Elvis and lured him into the trailer by scattering sweet-smelling corn and grain. Elvis, agreeable creature that he was, hopped right on.

When he was secured in the trailer, looking anxious and puzzled, I climbed up and gave him one last chocolate donut from Dunkin' Donuts, his favorite treat. I said goodbye, and thanks, and watched him looking back at me as the trailer lumbered up the road.

To this day, I still go out into the pasture where I would sit with Elvis and think about our time together.

When he saw me coming, he used to thunder down the hill. Since he couldn't always stop his gargantuan body when he wanted to, I would have to duck out of the way or risk being trampled. He loved to come up alongside me, snatch my hat off my head, and eat it. Several times he picked me up by the hood on my sweatshirt and dangled me like a toy until I swatted him on the nose and, startled and hurt, he dropped me.

I loved to sit up on the hill with him and look out at the valley and the other cows and farms down below. I often imagined Elvis thinking he had it pretty good up there. He had a girlfriend, Luna, a beef cow, for company, plenty of grass, fresh water, hay, and people who loved him.

When I visit Elvis's pasture, I like to think that he savored his life, but even if he didn't, or couldn't, I'm grateful that I gave him a few great years to live in comfort and ease.

Elvis's death was in some ways the beginning of my

adulthood, of knowing how to take care of myself and learning to make the choices I needed to make to live safely in the world. It was the beginning of a process that saved my farm from its worst crisis—my poor judgment and lack of responsibility—and allowed me to remain there. It returned the focus of my life to writing about dogs. It gave me confidence that I could face difficult things and resolve them and the courage to look everyone else squarely in the eye and say, "It was the right thing for me to do."

I gained perspective. I came to see what I could afford and what I couldn't, what would support my writing and what would threaten it. I learned that there had to be some limits to a life with animals. Elvis's death taught me about responsibility and judgment—both for my own life and for his.

Animal Dreams
ELVIS

In my dream, Elvis is standing at the top of the pasture.

His great big tail is swishing back and forth, warding off the big black flies that swarm around him from May to October.

He accepts this torment, as he does rain, snow, cold, and heat.

He loves to sit under the big old maple tree, by the old stone wall, looking down at the farms below.

I imagine you thought that you were very lucky, I tell him, to have all this space and grass. To be out of those big barns and away from the slaughterhouse. That you feel bad for all those cows and steers down in the field.

Is that what you're thinking?

No, not really, he says. *Those are human emotions. We accept our lives pretty much as they are. It was nice down there, and it's nice up here.*

Why is it, I ask, that you survived so long? And so many other cows and steers don't?

I learned to look human beings in the eye, he says.

Before:
Brace Yourself

SHORTLY AFTER MY DAUGHTER, Emma, was born, I got her a golden retriever puppy and named him Clarence after one of my heroes, the famed lawyer Clarence Darrow. I got Clarence for the wrong reasons at the wrong time and in the wrong way. I got him for a baby—which is just silly—when I was working as a television-news producer and rarely home, from a pet shop in a New Jersey strip mall.

He was ill-tempered, constantly nipping at children and fighting with other dogs, and riddled with so many skin allergies that I had to give him hyposensitizing injections three times a week.

Still, he was the first dog I had after Emma was born and the first I tried to train. I loved him quite a bit. Eight years later, when his kidneys gave out, I took him to a vet in Bloomfield, New Jersey, and sat with him as he was euthanized. On the way home I burst into tears and accidentally drove my car into a telephone pole.

This was one of my first lessons in grieving for an animal: be prepared.

Once I made the very difficult decision to euthanize Orson, I realized I had a lot of work to do. I couldn't just show up, watch him die, and expect to handle it well.

A few days before the appointment, I went to the vet's office. She explained the euthanasia procedure in detail so I could understand how it worked and picture the process.

I thought about whether I wanted or needed to be present. I decided I did want to be there—I owed Orson that, and I wanted to see him die peacefully so I didn't have to wonder whether he had suffered.

GOING HOME

I decided against bringing anyone else. He was my dog and had shaped my life. His death was my responsibility. I did ask a loyal friend to take me out for dinner later. I thought I would need a drink and wanted the companionship.

I made all the practical decisions about Orson's death. The vet offered to come to the farm, but I preferred that Orson receive the injection in her office where she had access to all of the necessary equipment should anything go wrong. I decided against cremation. I wanted to bury him on the farm where I could visit his grave, and where he could look out over the land, keep an eye on things, and maybe cause more havoc and mischief from beyond the grave, which I thought was likely.

The vet said she would put his body into a heavy plastic bag for transport. She would help me load it into my truck, and once I got home, I would carry Orson up the hill. I had the ATV ready in case I couldn't manage it. I called a handyman and asked him to dig a deep hole and to leave a shovel. I hired a mason to carve Orson's name on a headstone.

I ruled out any kind of postmortem or autopsy. It seemed excessive and inappropriate to me, although I would have agreed had the vet thought it could be useful in animal or veterinary research.

I called each of the vets who had treated him, two trainers who had helped me with him, and a holistic vet who had tried calming medications and acupuncture. I

| 53 |

told them of my decision. Most of them agreed that I had done everything possible, that Orson was damaged in ways that could probably not be helped by conventional or alternative veterinary medicine. I should feel no guilt, they said, and was making the right decision. One trainer disagreed vehemently, but she believed all animals should die a natural death and that was simply not a practical option for an aggressive dog like Orson.

I planned a private memorial service, to take place several days after his death up on the pasture where Orson would be buried. It would be attended by me and the other dogs who had lived with him—Rose and Clementine—and the rooster, Winston, who loved him.

I asked the people who knew and loved him to come by and say goodbye. When everyone had gone home, before we left for the vet's office, I sat with Orson and cried. I didn't want to do my grieving in public.

When we got to the vet's office, I was able to say goodbye to Orson in a calm and loving way. I knew what to expect when he died, and what would come next.

You're not going to be able to avoid grief by preparing for your dog's death, but being ready to face loss does help.

Euthanizing Orson wasn't easy, but at least I was prepared.

After:
Welcome Grief

GRIEF HURTS. BUT IT IS ALSO
healthy, even necessary. It is natural
and cleansing, a spiritual process as
well as a testament to the power of love
and attachment. As much as I dread
grief, I would hate to have a dog or cat
for whom I didn't grieve.

Grief is normal, inevitable, and unavoidable if you love your pet.

Expect it.

Accept it.

Embrace it, and allow it to take its course.

It will come, if you let it.

And then, after some time, it will go, if you let it.

In my own curious path toward adulthood and responsibility, I learned that anything worth doing is hard. Grieving, like many things, isn't easy, but with some work—both before and after the death of an animal—it doesn't have to be awful.

Izzy was a beautiful, well-bred border collie abandoned on a farm in Washington County, New York. He had lived mostly outside for years. An animal-rescue worker badgered me to go take a look at him. He was in rough shape, his hair matted with feces and burrs, his claws grown into talons. At first, Izzy was a wild creature. I thought he'd be untrainable. But a vet urged me to keep him. "He'll be a great dog for you."

The vet was right. When I became a hospice volunteer, Izzy came along for the training, and the two of us grew into a team. Izzy was a natural social worker. He took to hospice work immediately, always gentle and intuitive with the people we were visiting. Together we went into private homes, nursing homes, and hospitals. I was stunned by the bonds with people Izzy formed, by how loving he was, by how the terminally ill brightened at the sight of him and were so eager to tell him stories from their lives.

It wasn't pleasant to watch people die, but it wasn't entirely depressing either. Izzy and I found love, friendship, and profound connection visiting people on the edge of life. We laughed and cried in equal amounts. I learned a lot about grief and about the power of animals to lift our spirits and soothe our souls. My black Labrador, Lenore, also became a hospice dog, but her career was interrupted briefly (for further training) when the hamburgers and snacks of patients began to disappear.

The most important thing I learned in hospice work with Izzy is that death doesn't have to be depressing. It can be uplifting, beautiful, and enriching. I believe the same is true when it's time for an animal we love to leave us. Yes, it is painful, often a terrible loss. But it can also be a time of laughter and warmth, love and memory, tribute and recognition. This is true even when animals just disappear, leaving the humans who love them tormented by guilt and the lack of resolution.

I think of Angie, who took in the beautiful tortoiseshell cat who appeared at the door of her Vermont home one day. Merricat was an outdoor cat. She spent her days hunting and dancing in the woods. But every evening when Angie came home from work, Merricat was there waiting for her by the back door. She would snuggle next to Angie in front of the woodstove, so full of contradictions—at once loving and detached, aware and disconnected, domestic and wild. For nine years, the sweetest part of Angie's day was coming home to Merricat. And then one night the cat did not appear.

Angie put up posters, called vets, walked around in the cold and the rain calling for Merricat. She had visions of Merricat trapped out in the woods, injured, suffering, slowly dying. Coyotes, cars, dogs, foxes—any of these could have ended Merricat's life; it was the not knowing that tortured Angie. But after several weeks, she understood that Merricat was gone, and that she would never know what happened to her.

After much soul searching and talking with others, Angie realized that death is usually quick for animals. And that Merricat was too smart and savvy to have gotten herself stuck somewhere. Whatever took Merricat had to be swift and sure, and this gave Angie some comfort. As did accepting the idea that we can't know everything about creatures who are wild or partly wild. This is part of their mystery.

Finally, Angie was ready to say goodbye to Merricat. She took the blanket that Merricat had always curled up on in the house and walked out into the woods. She had prepared a eulogy for her cat and read it aloud, even though there wasn't another soul in sight:

"Merricat, goodbye. I need to bring my love for you and grief for you to a close, so that I can go on with my life and perhaps bring love and comfort to another cat. My guess is that you ran into some other creature of the night, one much like you, and that you sacrificed yourself for the freedom and independence you demanded, even as you loved me so much. I honor you for that, and love you for it. And so I say goodbye to you, right here and right now. I have mourned you, and I want to move ahead now. Your spirit will always be in my life, in my memory, and in these woods, where you lived your life on your own terms, and perhaps lost it in the same way. To you, I give all the love in the world."

Death is, for me, a spiritual experience. Perhaps the ultimate one. It defines us, our lives, as well as our sense of purpose and time.

When an animal of mine dies, I close my eyes and think of that animal leaving me. I think of Orson's fierce dedication to me, and his inability to live in a human world. Of Henrietta the hen's quirky personality and her refusal to be an ordinary chicken. Of Winston the rooster's gravitas, courage, and sense of duty. Of Elvis's genial companionship and affection. Of Stanley's journey with me from one phase of life to another. Sometime down the road, I will think of Izzy's grace in comforting the sick and the dying, and Rose's great professional ethic and sense of responsibility.

I mourn the loss of these creatures, but I also celebrate their spirits and honor them. It is a wonderful thing to love a dog or a cat, a bright and shining spot in a challenging world. I give thanks for it, however long my dog lives, and however painful it is to see him die. It is an awful and beautiful thing to grieve for an animal.

Through their deaths, I am opened to the love and light of the world, a final gift of feeling, a rebirth of understanding and meaning. Death is as much a part of life as birth.

In my grief over them, I see my other losses and sorrows. My sad and fearful childhood, my unhappy mother, my remote and disconnected father, the dreams I have lost and those I have found.

And I see my joy. The friends, the love, the challenges, the change. Is there a better way to learn and grow? From the darkness, light. From loss, gain. From sorrow, joy. To the animals I have loved and lost, I am nothing but grateful.

Pain defines love, gives it meaning. Without pain, love is nothing. Grieving hurts, but it cleanses and purifies us and brushes against our souls. It whispers to us that we received the great gift of unconditional love, and *that* does not ever die.

Grieving
Around Others

IF YOU ARE READING THIS BOOK, YOU
have likely lost an animal, or know
that you will soon. As you grieve for
your dog or cat, your friends and family members will try their best to support you. Some of the things they will
say will be helpful, but many will not.

It's important to understand that

most people *do* mean well, even if they don't say the right thing. According to the Argus Institute at Colorado State University College of Veterinary Medicine, when your pet dies you should expect to hear some dismissive platitudes, such as "There's no sense dwelling in the past." The institute's grief resources further explain: "These responses . . . encourage us to avoid our feelings and put pressure on us to get over the loss as soon as possible. . . . Everyone grieves in their own time and in their own way, and creating artificial deadlines or expecting grief to disappear overnight only creates more stress for the bereaved person."*

Try to not be angry when people say the wrong thing. In most cases they're trying to be helpful and just don't know any better.

Grieving is natural, and we all have to do it in our own way. Hospice work teaches this about grief: it is not our job to cheer people up or talk them out of their grief. Nor is it our job to tell anyone how to grieve. I have learned to be an "active listener," to meet people where they are, not where I might wish them to be. One learns quickly not to say, "Cheer up" or "Move on" or "Feel better." In hospice, things will not get better, and people have to mourn the people they love in their own very personal way, just as they must do with animals. Stuart's story illustrates this point well.

*www.argusinstitute.colostate.edu/understand.htm.

Stuart is a lawyer in his mid-fifties. He runs a small practice in Westchester County, New York, which deals mostly with matrimonial and real estate cases. He is a formal, ethical man, fastidious, orderly, and well organized. Although he dotes on his three children, now grown and scattered, Stuart's real emotional connection was with Gus, a twelve-year-old basset hound whom he and his wife had rescued from an animal shelter just before their youngest child went off to college.

One afternoon Stuart was watching the New York Giants play football and he let Gus out the back door into the fenced-in yard. Usually, Gus would do his business, then howl to be let in. He was not one of those dogs who liked to hang around outside in the dark or cold. He liked sofas and carpets and his eighty-nine-dollar L.L. Bean cedar-chip-stuffed bed.

But when some time passed and Stuart didn't hear the usual howl, he got up and looked outside. Gus was lying on his side, absolutely still. Stuart ran outside, but even as he did he knew that Gus had passed, almost surely as a result of the congestive heart failure the vet predicted would take him one day.

Stuart was inconsolable. He felt the most severe pain and sadness. And guilt. Could he have done something? Could Gus have lived longer?

Weeks and months passed, and Stuart still felt the loss acutely—when he got up in the morning, when he came home at night, when he watched TV. It was not something Stuart would ever have said or thought about a dog, but he had this unaccountable feeling that he had lost his best friend.

After a year, Stuart was alarmed by the fact that his feelings of sadness and loss had not lessened appreciably. He still thought of Gus, still missed him, still felt a stab in the heart. Was this normal, he wondered? He was a rational man, a man of law, not one of these animal nuts. Gus was just a dog, after all.

One day, browsing on the Internet at work, checking out basset hound websites and blogs—something he had done almost daily since Gus had died—he saw an advertisement for a pet-grieving hot line. Stuart had never in his life asked for any kind of psychological or emotional help. He hadn't even discussed Gus's death much with his wife, let alone a total stranger. But almost without thinking, he picked up the phone and dialed.

A man answered on the second ring.

"You're going to think I'm crazy," Stuart told the man on the other end, "but my basset hound, Gus, died a year ago. And I'm just still so sad about it. . . ." Stuart was horrified to hear himself choking up, stifling a sob, struggling to get control of himself. Lord, he thought, what is happening to me?

The man on the other end was gentle, patient, soothing.

"Take your time," he said, "I'm not in a rush." Stuart could hear phones ringing in the background, other voices. He was glad nobody had asked for his name, but the man said his name was Steve.

"Don't worry about it," Steve said. "A lot of people feel this way." He told Stuart that his feelings were perfectly normal, perfectly natural. And, of course, men experienced them as well as women.

"I know you can't go into the office and tell people you're all torn up over a basset hound," said Steve. "They might think you're crazy. But you're not, you're just sad, and it helps to say so, to know it's a wonderful thing to be sad over an animal you loved."

When Stuart got off the phone, he sobbed and sobbed, tears streaming down his cheeks. He locked his inner office door so his secretary wouldn't see or hear him. He wrote the number of Steve's direct line on a memo pad and stuffed it into the desk drawer. He didn't want his wife to find it, lest she think he was having an affair. But for the first time in a long while, Stuart felt better.

Our culture does not want to deal with death, loss, or grief. People avoid it, discourage it, flee from it. We are encouraged to hide grief, as if it were shameful, rather than deal with it more forthrightly. As a consequence, those who are dealing with death and loss do not have an understanding environment in which to grieve.

You must allow yourself to mourn, but given our society's reaction to this, consider withholding your grief in some workplaces and around some people. Few companies take animal grieving seriously, at least at this point. After all, you're unlikely to get a few weeks of paid bereavement time to mourn your dog. Roughly half of Americans don't own a dog or a cat, and believe me, most of those people just won't understand what you're going through. Our views of animals in America are evolving, but not that much and not that quickly. Woe to a politician who falls apart grieving his cat on a cable talk show. Like it or not, non-animal lovers, and even some animal owners, are quick to brand people as weird if they show too much grief over the loss of an animal.

This might not be fair, but it is the nature of our society. Expecting everyone in the real world to understand your grief for a dead pet can set you up for embarrassment and disappointment. Grieve in a safe and appropriate space, among people you trust.

Where might you find such a place?

Perhaps you have good friends who have lost a pet or there is someone in your family sensitive enough to listen without judgment while you talk through your feelings of sadness. Some people are empathetic, some are not. If you are uneasy sharing your grief with anyone close to you, there is a powerful new tool for finding comfort during a difficult time: the Internet.

Yes, the Net is a wild, chaotic, and sometimes hostile place, but there are all kinds of virtual communities within it that can be sources of encouragement, support, and sympathy. Search engines help us find these groups instantly. Pet lovers are intensely communicative. They love to share stories, photos, and experiences—such as grief—online.

Of course, technology is not a substitute for human beings and human affection. But sometimes anonymity makes it easier to be honest and open and to find the people who understand what you're feeling. I think we all fear vulnerability and ridicule, never more so than when a pet we love dies and we are torn up about it.

Animal-related mailing lists and blogs can fuse people and technology in a way that can be extraordinarily helpful when a pet dies. A woman emailed me that she was having a rough time when her eleven-year-old beagle and "best chum," Nellie, died. Her husband told her, "Nellie was a good dog, but she was just a dog. You need to move on." He was clearly annoyed. Not wanting trouble in her marriage, she found a beagle blog online and posted about her loss. By morning, she had more than a hundred messages of understanding, sympathy, and support. "I guess I realized that I wasn't a jerk for loving this dog or missing her. I wish my husband had known that, but even so, I got the help I needed."

In my own life with animals, I have found support, understanding, and encouragement online. After months of grieving for Orson, I had a turning point one morning when the farm was engulfed in a full-blown winter storm, drifts piling up almost to the windows. I had gone out with Rose to feed the sheep and donkeys and slog through the snow. I came in, fired up the woodstove, warmed up, but somehow couldn't settle. My grief was completely distracting. I went online and, without giving my real name, posted this message on a dog lovers website:

"I put my dog down after he bit and hurt three people. It was a few months ago, but I feel pretty awful."

I thought of it as a message sent out into the ether. I had no expectation of reply. A few minutes later, I saw that messages were pouring into my in-box. A rodeo hand in Wyoming told me that he also had to euthanize an aggressive dog, and it was the worst thing he had ever felt. An analyst in Chicago told me she was grieving over her sweet pit bull, and none of her friends could understand why she loved a pit bull in the first place, not to mention her feelings of loss. A high school art teacher two towns away in Upstate New York emailed me that it took her a long time to get over the loss of her golden retriever. Later that evening I opened a message from a writer and naturalist in Wisconsin. "I think I know who you are," she wrote. "And I wanted to tell you this. You are a good man, and you will heal up and move on, as any dog worth anything would want you to do." I appreciated that. And she was right. I did heal up and move on.

Helping Yourself, Helping Others

I'M FREQUENTLY ASKED WHAT *I* SAY to people who have lost a dog or a cat.

What do I say when an animal dies?

I say: "I'm sorry. I know how you feel. I know it's very hard."

Your own loss will help you be there for others when it's their time to grieve. I'm not suggesting that you react to the death of someone else's animal by talking about the dog or cat who *you* lost. That is not, to me, appropriate or helpful. People do not need to experience our losses when they're going through their own. They should not feel pressured to comfort you when their own grief is so immediate.

But once you've lost an animal you love, you will be more sympathetic to others who experience loss. Consider what was helpful to you, and follow these guidelines.

1. Listen. Actively. Sometimes the most comforting words are no words.
2. Say you are sorry.
3. Don't manage the grief of others or try to take it away. Don't tell them when or if it's time to move on and feel better.
4. Don't trivialize their experience by saying things like "It's just a dog," or "There are lots of dogs," or "Your dog had a better life than most people."
5. Be supportive. People often say, "I'm not a nut, but I'm devastated." Tell them they are not strange or crazy. Assure them that it's natural to grieve a dog or cat, that it hurts, but that it's okay to take it seriously, to cry, to take care of themselves.
6. If the grieving seems destructive—if it goes on for months, interferes with daily functioning, or triggers severe depression for long periods—then it

might be a good idea to suggest that they seek professional help.

Sometimes the right thing to say is very simple.

One cold winter night, Rose and I were out in the pasture during lambing. It was windy, snowing, and difficult to see. Barking anxiously, Rose tore up the hill, and when I had climbed up through the mud and ice I saw my oldest ewe, Number 43, fighting to give birth. Something was wrong. Her uterus was dry, suggesting that her amniotic sac had burst sometime earlier.

There was no time to call for a vet, and it was too late at night to get ahold of one anyway. Rose backed up and watched me as I reached into the birth canal and after some struggle pulled the lamb out. It was alive, but barely. I gave the lamb a vitamin and energy shot, cleared the mucus from its nose and face, and cut the umbilical cord. Then I massaged the lamb and gave it another shot, preparing to get it into the barn and under a heat lamp.

The snow cleared and bright moonlight filled the pasture. Rose whined, and touched the ewe with her nose. I saw instantly that she was dead. The lamb uttered a soft cry, and then its head drooped down, hanging lifelessly in my arms.

I felt a wave of sorrow, guilt, and helplessness. Rose turned away, looking for another lamb, another birth. I kept staring at the open eyes of the lamb in my arms, then down at the ewe.

I couldn't move, not for many minutes.

Then I went into the farmhouse and called a neighbor, a farmer who had given me his number in case of an emergency.

His big pickup pulled into the farm just a few minutes later, and he got out of his truck with a burlap bag and an enormous flashlight. He saw me right away, standing by the ewe, the lamb once again in my arms.

He came over and took the lamb from me, placed it into the bag, then brought it over to his truck. He pulled the dead ewe over as well and put it in the bed next to the lamb. Then he took my arm, walked me into the house, and asked me if I had any liquor. I had some scotch and he poured each of us a glass.

He raised his glass and toasted. "To life and death," he said. "I'm sorry. It always hurts."

There was nothing else to be said, really. And it helped.

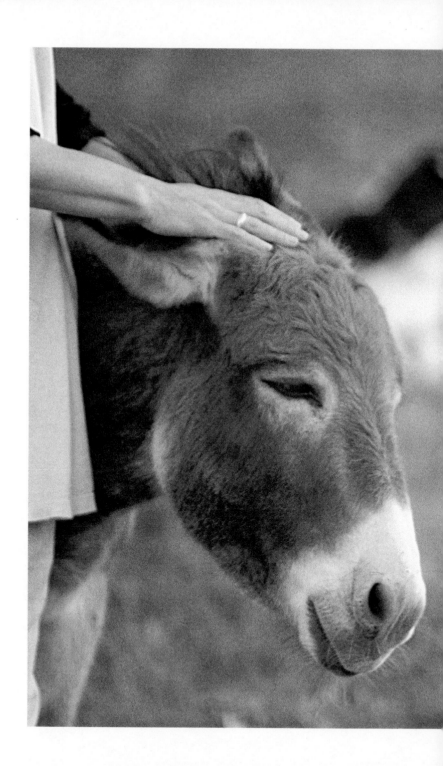

Grieving and Healing Through Stories

OUR CULTURE IS AWASH IN FAUX sensitivity. There is a lot of what I call "smooth and thin" advice out there that purports to help people through the grieving process. I spent several days exploring animal-bereavement pamphlets and animal websites and found remarkably similar prescriptions:

Acknowledge your grief and give yourself permission to express it.

Write about your feelings.

Contact local pet-support groups.

Call a pet-loss hot line.

These suggestions makes sense and are helpful to many, but for some of us they don't go deep enough or reflect our individual experience when we give a dog or cat away, see one die, or put one down. They seem inadequate to express the very personal nature of our loss.

I have found that grieving is so personal, and our relationships with our dogs and cats so individualistic, that telling the stories of the animals we have loved and lost can help. There are lots of ways to do this. On blogs, websites, message boards, and mailing lists. Through poems, songs, journals, or photographs. No matter what the medium, you will find a way to tell your story.

One of the most inspired strategies for grieving and healing was shared with me by a woman named Fran, who had struggled for two years to move past the loss of her border collie, Daisy, her companion and soul mate for twelve years. "Daisy left a huge hole in my life. I missed her every day, in the most painful way. It astonished me, the depth of it. I needed to do something. For me, loving dogs isn't about feeling badly. Just the opposite. This isn't something Daisy would have wanted. I remembered that I always sang to Daisy, almost every morning. Most of the time, she would sing right back to me. The two of us would be there in the kitchen howling happily, sometimes even dancing. How can you not love a dog like that?

"So when I was grieving the most for Daisy, a process so painful I cannot even begin to describe it, I decided to sing to her again, every morning, until it got better. I'm not sure why, but this helped so much. I know so many dog lovers who sing to their dogs. Why not now, when it matters the most?

"The song I sang to Daisy every morning was 'You Are My Sunshine,' and I decided to sing that to her again, hoping that wherever she was, she would hear it, lay her ears back, wag her tail and look at me, then break into a howl and whine of her own. Some things don't ever die. This is one of the versions I sing to her, softly, with my eyes closed and my heart wide open. It really helped me, though not without a lot of tears:

"You are my Daisy, my only Daisy.
You make me happy
when I am sad.
You always knew, dog,
how much I loved you,
and how it hurt
when you went away.
The other night, love,
while it was storming,

I dreamed I held you in my arms,
When I awoke, girl,
I was mistaken,
And I just closed my eyes and
cried.
You are my Daisy.
My only Daisy.
You made me happy,
when I was sad.
I think you knew me,
as no one knew me.
But they took my Daisy away.
I'll always love you
and sing my songs, too,
though you can't
come back to me.
You always knew, girl,
how much I loved you.
And they can never
take that away."

Like fingerprints, no two stories of loving an animal are alike. Each dog and cat is different, and each sparks different emotions in us, different responses. Some animals help us to be more loving and patient, some drive us crazy and challenge us to be better people.

I think about Orson riding across the country with me, sticking his head out the car window. About Rose and me up in the pasture, moving sheep. About Lenore lying at the foot of my bed as I nearly drowned in loneliness and fear, forcing a smile from me whenever she turned those sad eyes my way. And about Izzy, my hospice therapy dog, who helped people leave the world with comfort, dignity, and grace as I watched in awe.

To me, these stories are sacred.

When the time comes to say goodbye to an animal, I find a way to tell his or her story, and that helps me channel my loss and grief in a meaningful way.

When my Lab Stanley died in New Jersey, I had his body cremated and decided to hold a memorial service for him. I scattered his ashes in the backyard and collected a pile of his favorite bones and balls.

My daughter, Emma, spoke about him and how much she loved cuddling with him in bed.

A neighbor came by with her own Lab and told me how much she appreciated Stanley's good nature, and how much her dog, Ginger, loved playing with him.

I talked about Stanley's adaptation to the writing life, when I left a corporate media job and came home to write. He began sleeping under my desk, keeping me company as I adapted to working alone. We would take walks together, during which I thought about my work and honed my ideas. Those walks were a creative lubricant and provided a time and space for me to organize my scattered thoughts.

He did not, of course, understand what a writing career meant, yet he slipped gracefully and lovingly into my new life.

So on that day, I read aloud a few of the first paragraphs of one of my first books, written with him at my side (or by my feet), and I thanked him for helping me make this transition. A writer's life, I said, can be lonely. He kept me company and helped me get used to it while serving as a foot warmer in my cold basement.

I told the story of how Stanley once dropped his ball into a sewer and looked for it every day through a long winter. One day in the spring, he barked and looked up at me—the ball had popped up in a storm drain, on the street where we often walked. I lay down with the scooper and reached into the drain to try to retrieve the ball. It was raining and the ball was several feet down from the street level; grasping it was a struggle. Eventually one of the neighbors called the police, assuming I had had a heart attack or other misadventure.

The patrol car screeched up along with an ambulance, and the officers looked down at me in a concerned way. I explained what I was doing, and incredulous, they got back into their patrol car, one policeman shaking his head and saying to the other: "I wish I were his dog."

Stanley was loved.

Animal Dreams
STANLEY

In my dream, Stanley is sitting in a field of rubber balls, and they are bouncing all around him. He rolls in them, and chases them, drops them into holes, growls and barks and leaps for joy.

When he sees me, he stops, wags his

tail, and then rushes to me, showering me with licks, bumping his head into me, sniffing me.

Hey, he says. *It's great to see you.* He drops a ball on the ground in front of me, waiting for me to throw it. Balls are rolling and bouncing everywhere.

What was your purpose in my life? I ask.

To make you laugh. To keep fun alive for you. To make you smile. And step out of yourself.

That's all?

That's a lot.

So it was that simple? You kept laughter alive for me?

A dozen times a day.

I threw the ball and he tore off after it. I smiled.

Guilt

IF YOU'RE READING THIS BOOK, YOU adore your dog or your cat. You treat your animal gently and lovingly. You feed him well and play with him. You rush him to the vet for the best care when he is sick. Now that your pet is gone, you have nothing to feel guilty about. You have done nothing wrong.

Guilt serves no purpose, for you or for your dog. Do not taint your loving relationship with so small and petty a human emotion as guilt, a feeling dogs are so far beyond.

Guilt is not an animal emotion. It exists solely in the flawed realm of human beings. Dogs are not as complex as we are. They lack many of our more destructive tendencies—envy, spite, greed, propensity for violence, contempt for the environment, wastefulness. Dogs use what they need and leave the rest behind. They do not war on one another or on other species. They do not know vengeance or hatred. Or guilt.

Guilt is ours alone. It is one of the many things that plagues the complicated human psyche but does not infect the life of an animal. Dogs do not feel guilty for eating the last piece of food or for hogging the bed. They do not reproach themselves for making mistakes. They do not blame themselves when we suffer, struggle, or die.

In turn, dogs accept their own fates. They are not astonished by the realities of life. They do not blame other living things for their suffering, troubles, or death. They do not resent us for failing to offer miracles. They are both wiser and simpler than that.

Guilt is a toxic emotion, out of place in the symbiotic and devoted relationship between us and animals. It has no place in the fabled history of people and dogs. It was never part of the timeless contract between human beings and the animals that share their lives, a relationship built on love, service, care, nurturing, and companionship. We love and care for animals, and they love us back without qualification. They protect us, keep us company, and touch the deepest parts of ourselves. They enter our lives at critical points and go when they must.

Guilt isn't part of the deal.

I struggled with guilt when I put Orson down. And when I sent Elvis to market. But not for long, and not now. I loved these animals and gave them healthy food, good medical care, shelter, and affection. Guilt has no place crawling in between my love of these animals and their love of me. It corrodes something that is beautiful.

When it comes to making decisions about animals in distress or at the end of their lives, guilt seems to be the silent partner, the unacknowledged elephant in the room. It is a powerful force, one I hope you will manage to avoid.

Guilt is tied to the decisions we make. In fact, the more decisions we make about the death of our dogs and cats, the more likely we are to feel guilty about them. Should we have tried more medication? Another surgery? Spent more money? Tried another vet? Waited?

These decisions are tough. Despite all of the books and websites and blogs, when it comes to making choices about the deaths of our animals, we are on our own. We never will know for sure if the decisions we make are the right ones. That's the lonely truth of it. There is no one—

no force, no expert, no guru—who can tell us that we did the right thing. We must convince ourselves of that.

There are no reliable statistics on how many dogs die a natural death and how many are euthanized, but most of us feel differently about a dog who dies in his or her sleep than we do about one we decide to put down. A natural death seems easier because we are spared making a heart-breaking decision.

Still, I know a lot of people who beat themselves up anyway. Was there something they should have done or noticed?

A friend called me after she found her beloved cairn terrier, Lucy, dead on the kitchen floor when she came home from work. "Last night she didn't lick me the way she usually does when I come home. I should have noticed that, should have known something was wrong."

I tried to persuade my friend not to blame herself. Nobody would ever know why Lucy didn't lick her as usual, and did it really, in the long run, matter? Would it have altered the course of things?

My friend had loved Lucy, and had been loved deeply in return. Lucy had had a good life and a peaceful death. Couldn't that be enough?

For some people it is enough. For others, it is almost impossible to reconcile the death of a pet with an acute sense of failure; they believe that the death is their fault in some way.

This is sad. And it's not true. This is not the story of

our lives with these precious creatures, not the real ending.

If you are reading this, your heart is likely to be broken, and you are awash in grief and loss. Trust me, sad reader, when I tell you that a life with a dog or cat is a lifetime of decisions. Cast away guilt and remind yourself that you did the best you could. This attitude will preserve the wonderful relationship you had with your pet and help you begin to heal.

Saying
Goodbye

I WRESTLED WITH ORSON'S DEATH
for a long time. I couldn't seem to get a
handle on it. I wanted to know that he
had forgiven me. I wanted to know
that it was okay. And so I turned to an
animal communicator.

For me to even be speaking with an
animal communicator was not some-

thing I ever expected or imagined. I pride myself on being a rationalist. But I have learned some powerful truths in my life with animals, especially in the wake of their loss. I now recognize that there are many things beyond my understanding, many things I cannot see, but that doesn't mean these things aren't real.

Like many men, I needed to be shocked and jarred into consciousness, into understanding my own emotions and the spiritual nature of the world. The death of many animals I have loved served as those shocks, helping me evolve more fully as a human being. Each death, in its own way, was also a magnet, drawing me closer to the mystical parts of nature and life.

The animal communicators I have encountered know things they could not know if they did not possess powers and instincts that I do not have. It's as simple as that, and as complex.

When Julius and Stanley died, I wouldn't have considered listening to an animal communicator. But by the time I'd been on Bedlam Farm a few years, seeing so much of life and death, it seemed both a natural and comfortable thing to me.

I asked my friend Lesley, an animal communicator and shaman, to come to the farm and look for Orson's spirit. She sat with me, burned incense, lit candles, and then closed her eyes and chanted. She said that she came to a river where Orson was waiting for her. There were blue lights everywhere. His appearance meant that he wished to talk with me.

Orson told Lesley that he was not gone. He checked up on me occasionally. He blamed me for nothing; he'd had a good life and had left when it was his time. He was ready to go.

"When he comes to see me, what does he do?" I asked.

Speaking softly, Lesley said that he lay on the floor in the study with his head on my foot while I wrote. A shiver went up my spine. I frequently felt pressure on my right foot when I sat at the computer. In fact, I felt it so often that I constantly looked down to see if something was lying on my shoe. Lesley didn't know that. Nobody did. To this day, I still occasionally feel that pressure, and I know that Orson has come to say hello.

She told me that Orson was worried about Winston, my venerable old rooster who was slowing down with age and losing his powerful voice. Lesley saw that Orson and Winston had been close to each other. It was true. The two were always either together or looking for each other. They were the oddest couple on the farm. Lesley could not have known this either.

I am no sage, no dog whisperer. As a writer and photographer, I don't often drift from what I can see. I live on a farm, in the real and very practical world. But I believe what Lesley told me. I believe that Orson is not dead in the sense that I understand the word. I know he comes to see me. To watch over me. To tell me he's all right. When I feel his invisible weight on my foot, I close my eyes and think of him in the place by the river, a spirit among all those blue lights.

I learned that day that there are things about animals we don't understand and cannot know. We think we know our animals. We believe that they think the way we think and feel what we feel. This is hubris. In some ways, they are so far beyond us.

Animals smell things we don't smell, see things we don't see, hear things we don't hear. Their instincts are beyond anything we have or know, and they experience things we can only begin to imagine. By assuming that they're like us, we diminish them, when the truth is that they have gifts and abilities that we simply cannot grasp.

We humans are the only species believed to know that we are dying, and to fear it above almost all other things. And in the same way that we imagine our pets experiencing loneliness, guilt, or any of the other complex emotions unique to human beings, we expect that the animals we love are aware of death, and fear it.

Yet I have sat with many animals—dogs, cats, ewes, lambs, cows, chickens, and a rooster—when they died. I see in them not fear but something else, something profoundly spiritual, something calm. I see acceptance. In this sense, they are so much more evolved than we are.

A dog doesn't die like a human. He doesn't ask for more medication, seek different health care, enter a nursing home or a hospital, express regret and fear, or seek out the company of loved ones. We are stunned by death and loss, as if we never imagined we would experience them. We deny death, stave it off, tear ourselves up over it. The animals we love don't do that. They come when they're needed, leave when they're done, and go, I believe, to a place beyond my imagination.

Understanding how the death of animals is different from that of humans does not make the loss of them any less painful or difficult, but it does change the context of their death and remind us not to do animals the disservice of thinking of them as human beings. I don't know where they go when they die, but when Lesley described her world of blue lights and peaceful waters, I could see it and it seemed right to me, and beautiful, a fitting place for creatures with a consciousness so different from our own.

When I buried Orson on that sticky August day, I did not say goodbye to him. There's a difference between burying someone you love and saying goodbye, although I didn't know that at the time. Leaving something so important unfinished weighed on me.

Just before I began writing this book, Rose and I walked up to the top of the hill. I've visited Orson every few days since I buried him, but Rose rarely goes up to the grave on her own. Once in a while, I look up and see her sitting at the top of the pasture, near the marker but looking away from it. I can't say what she's doing up there. When we go up together, Rose always sniffs Orson's grave and lies down.

On that visit, I stood over Orson's marker and bowed my head, listening to the wind. I looked at the sun rolling through clouds and over the beautiful valley.

Rose watched me as I said:

"Orson, I wanted to come up here and give you a proper goodbye. I'm sorry you didn't stay with me longer. I miss you. You meant the world to me, and you changed my life. I owe you much. I want you to know that I did the best I could for you, and I'm learning that the best I can do has to be enough sometimes, even when it doesn't work out the way I want.

"I want you to know that my life has changed, and that I have moved on. I have new dogs that I love, and they fill many of the holes that I had in my life and my heart. I have a new woman in my life as well. Maria. You would have loved her very much. She would have loved you, too, and perhaps even helped you more than I could. I wanted to say a simple goodbye, and to thank you. I didn't do it when you died, and I owed it to both of us. I wish you a safe and happy journey."

As I said those words, I could almost feel some of the guilt and grief lift out of me, up into the air, and across the pasture. I felt—I was—lighter, better.

It's important to say goodbye. If you can't do it when your dog or cat dies, you can do it later—but be sure to do it. You can do it anytime, anywhere. More than once. Even right now.

This morning, writing this, I closed my eyes and thought of Orson. I remembered his first herding trial, during which the sheep shocked the judge by jumping over the fence and running off into the woods to hide. I thought of the time he herded a neighbor's Yorkie and drove it into our backyard, and the time he tried to herd a school bus. I grabbed him and dragged him over to the bushes at the side of the road, cursing at him, then laughing, then taking his head in my arms and kissing him on the nose.

I think of the glorious history of people and dogs, living with and loving one another for thousands of years. That history is so much bigger than me, and bigger than Orson, and it gives me a sense of perspective that makes me feel better.

Goodbye, Orson, I say to myself. You were a pain in the ass.

No matter how often I bid him goodbye, I still cry sometimes. Not as much anymore, but a little.

I felt Orson's spirit brush against me again one winter night in the barn when his friend Winston lay dying beneath the roosting hens he watched over so vigilantly.

It was an eerie, almost beautiful scene. The night was quiet, still. The big barn was dark, save for a heat lamp. Winston had barely moved in two days and I had placed him on a bed of straw in a crate, to protect him from predators and the hens, who sometimes attacked their ill brethren. Minnie, one of my barn cats, adored Winston and often slept near him at night. While he was ill, she lay by his side, rubbing against him.

Winston had had a good run for a rooster. He was the symbol of my farm. He woke me up every morning at four o'clock with a bone-rattling crow and screeched loudly at odd and surprising times throughout the day, for no discernible reasons. When I didn't think of shooting him to quiet the racket, I admired him greatly.

I had adopted Winston from another farm. A hawk had attacked the chickens, and though the other rooster fled, Winston stayed to defend his hens. His leg was mangled by the hawk. He moved into semiretirement at my farm, a quieter place, where he had only three hens to supervise. He did his job with great authority and vigilance, even standing off with my dogs if they came too close to a chicken, which they quickly learned not to do.

And he loved Orson, which was perhaps a harder job than protecting the hens.

Winston didn't seem to know he was impaired, and I

loved the sight of him puffing himself up and hobbling all over the farm. He had climbed up the pasture the day I buried Orson, trying to see what was going on, looking for his friend. Every now and then I saw him there, hanging around the grave. After a few months, he seemed to move on. Now it was his turn. A farm is a never-ending cycle of life and death, rebirth and loss. After a while, you come to see this as not a tragic but as an integral part of life. Death makes life meaningful.

That night in the barn, Winston's eyes were closing, his breathing slowing. He was close. He was no longer taking food or water. Despite the stillness of the evening, I felt a soft breeze sweep through the barn, circle me, and lift the feathers on Winston's tail.

I knew that Orson had come back to show himself to me and to take Winston to the other side, as he had told Lesley he would. Finally, we had said goodbye to each other.

This is a story with a happy ending. Orson's death turned out to be a gift as well as a loss. My love for him was elemental, pure. So was his affection for me. It was not complicated by human dramas and emotions—arguments, boundaries, passions, and differences. When you lose a dog or cat, you lose love, plain and simple. Love is hard to come by in our world, and love you get every day, no strings attached, is precious. We open ourselves up to dogs and cats in ways we rarely do with people, and when we lose them, we lose that trust and connection.

But Orson's death taught me what an animal can mean to a person like me. I have struggled all of my life to deal with loss, love, and connection. His death helped me to be more open, and to respect myself. It taught me the futility of guilt and the importance of trusting my decisions. I learned how to say goodbye. The loss of Orson showed me the power and depth of love. And my need for it.

I have come to see the death of an animal as very different from the death of a human. I miss Orson every day, but his presence in my life has not only continued beyond that August day but has flowered and grown, as I have.

I could finally see it. Orson had come for a reason and left when his time was over.

Perspective

ONE LATE-SPRING MORNING MY WIFE, Maria, and I were just waking up when I heard a piercing sound coming from the pasture behind the farm-house. We had agreed to take in some sheep from a Vermont farmer for the coming summer. I would have sheep to work with Rose, they would have fresh grass to eat, and the farmer's grass would be left to grow for winter hay. He would come to collect the sheep before the weather turned cold.

It was a good arrangement all around.

Sometimes the ewes would call out to one another, but this was a different sound, more urgent and high-pitched.

"It sounds like a lamb," I told Maria. I had lambed on the farm five or six times and I knew the shrill call of a baby looking for its mother.

This was a surprise; we hadn't known any of the sheep were pregnant, and neither had Darryl, the farmer.

Maria and I found the newborn boy in the Pole Barn, quite alone and yelling to bring the sky down. His mother was conspicuously absent. That was a bad sign. Sheep bond by smell, and right away; if they don't manage to do that, they might not bond at all and the lamb would have to be bottle-fed.

I called Rose, and she rushed up the hill and went straight to the mother, a black ewe with afterbirth still dangling from her backside.

Maria picked up the lamb and carried him to a small training pen in the pasture. He was still yowling for his mother, but the ewe was unresponsive. As Rose drove her toward the training pen, the ewe tried to break away, but Maria tackled her and dragged her into the pen. Sometimes, if you get an unresponsive mother and her lamb together soon enough after birth, they will figure things out. It was worth a try.

As unprepared as we were to have a new lamb, Maria and I threw ourselves into fostering a bond between the two animals. We got the two of them into the barn and into a cozy, hay-stuffed lambing pen. We checked the mother's teats for milk. We held her still so the lamb could get enough to eat. We visited them at night and brought fresh water and hay.

Not only did his mother bond with him but the other ewes accepted the lamb too, and even mothered and nuzzled him a bit. He bonded with Lulu, one of my donkeys. He thrived. Saving a life is a profound experience, no matter what form that life takes.

Maria thought the lamb was cute and almost immediately named him Bartleby, after the main character in Melville's short story "Bartleby the Scrivener." We both thought it was touching that the lamb and his mother had formed such a strong connection, despite the rocky start.

I made Bartleby's struggle to survive a running (and very popular) story on my blog. I spent hours crawling around the pasture with my zoom lens, looking for the perfect angles from which to capture this heartwarming drama. I chronicled Bartleby's every move with dozens of adorable photographs. I loved photographing the lamb, who was so at ease around the camera. Within days he had a large following on the Internet, and I was startled to get a lot of emails urging—demanding—that I keep him on the farm.

On some level, I knew we had crossed a line. I knew

that cute lambs become aggressive rams, and that names like "Bartleby" accelerate the personification of animals. When you name a cute lamb, take photos of him— Bartleby nestled with his mom, Bartleby making friends with other farm animals, Bartleby sniffing flowers in the pasture—and then post those photos on your blog, you are setting in motion the very human process of attachment. But I couldn't help it, really. So Bartleby became something other than a sheep.

He was a sort of surrogate farm child. We were projecting all sorts of sweet ideas onto his life and psyche— that he was grateful to us for saving him, that he loved us, that he enjoyed hanging out with the donkeys. We had altered his identity. He was no longer a farm animal; he had become a human creation. He was now a character in a fairy tale.

Because I write animal stories for a living, a story like that was almost irresistible. But instinctively, I came to see that the story couldn't have a happy ending. Soon, it would be time to send Bartleby away. He would no longer be a cute little lamb; he'd be a grumpy, hungry, smelly, and possibly dangerous ram. Bartleby was not a child or even a pet; he was a farm animal.

A few years ago, one of my lambs was rejected by his mother. A neighbor fell in love with him and begged to take him. She bottle-fed him and brought him into the kitchen on cold winter nights. He had no idea how to behave as a pet and could not be housebroken or trained.

But neither did he know how to behave as a sheep anymore. The other sheep on my neighbor's farm did not accept him and constantly butted him. I heard that she kept him in a spare bedroom for several months so that he'd be safe from the other animals. When I ran into her at the store one day, she told me he had gotten so large and unruly that she had eaten him for Christmas dinner. The symbolism was not lost on me. Sometimes we make our own grief, and sometimes, when we lose perspective, we make a lot of it.

One morning, just after I'd posted another photo of Bartleby on my blog, Maria and I went for a walk in the woods. "You know, it would be a mistake for us to keep Bartleby," I said. "He's not ours, for one thing. He's surely not going to be kept as a pet on the farm he came from, and in a few months he'll be a big ram, needing lots of hay and wanting nothing to do with people or cameras."

We both agreed that Bartleby needed to go back to Vermont when the farmer came to pick up his sheep. We didn't know what his fate would be, but we understood that he would likely go to market, because that was what the farmer did. That was how he made his living.

We began to adjust our perspective. Bartleby stopped being an endearing symbol of the perfect life and became an animal again.

I stopped taking photos of him. Maria stopped visiting

him. We left him to his life as a sheep, out in the pasture with the others. It was not his destiny to be a pet, nor was it appropriate, it seemed to me.

Once we stopped calling him Bartleby and painting our own stories on this living canvas, we both noticed that our feelings for him had changed. He was no longer our cute little pet. He was a sheep. We would miss him—we had brought him into the world—but we had altered course. We would not grieve him.

A dog or cat is different from a lamb, of course, but it's still important to keep things in perspective when you're grieving the loss of an animal you love. The grief cannot be avoided. But perspective—the way in which we choose to understand their deaths—can soften our loss and ease our pain. With perspective, we can, to some degree, shape the process of grief.

We all write our own stories about the animals we love. We tell ourselves that they know us, love us, understand us. Miss us when we go to work. Would pine for us if we were gone. Animals cannot tell us we are wrong, or walk away, or roll their eyes in disgust. We can make them anything we want them to be. This is one reason we love them so much, and mourn them so much when they're gone. Why we sometimes feel the loss of them more acutely than the loss of people we love.

Our relationships with animals are simple and pure.

They are free of the conflict, drama, cruelty, and disappointment that so often mar our connections with human beings. People are more complicated than animals, and so, inevitably, is loving and mourning them.

Dogs herd sheep, rescue people, do hospice and therapy work, sniff out bombs. But perhaps their most significant work in the world today is to fill the gaps in our emotional lives. When money runs out. When work is insecure. When families scatter to the winds. When children leave us. When friends betray us. When religion fails to uplift us. When politics fail to inspire us.

We seem to love animals more and more all the time, especially as we find it more difficult to connect with the people and institutions that have always sustained us.

Dogs and cats heal us when nothing else can.

Animals support us. They provide us with emotional nourishment of the most basic and elemental kind. As our love for animals grows, so does the depth and pain of our grief when they die. And it can be too easy to lose perspective. The idea that animals should never be put down or killed—an idea that would have astounded our predecessors at any point in history—has become popular in America. The idea of any animal dying has become nearly unbearable, and so we believe we must keep our pets alive at any cost.

A farm quickly puts things in perspective. There is no such thing as a no-kill farm. A farmer who refuses to kill an animal will not be a farmer for long. He will be a zookeeper or the owner of an animal-rescue facility. He will be broke.

The farmer's life is a struggle. A farm is a cycle of seasons, and of life and death. I am reminded of this every day. When coyotes snatch chickens and kill deer. When sheep eat poisoned weeds. When lambs die. When dogs grow old and need to be put down. When barn cats snatch barn swallows out of the sky and torture and kill them. When foxes run down rabbits and owls snatch chipmunks right off the ground. When the legs of steers give out and they fall to the ground, never to get up.

When I first moved to Bedlam Farm, a farmer from the nearby town of Cossayuna came by and offered me some advice that I thought was strange at the time.

"Listen," he said. "If you are going to be a farmer, get used to life and death. They both exist together. They are two ends of the same thing. You may love your animals, but you will need people to survive. You can't call a border collie when lightning hits your house or the fence has broken through. The farm comes first, and everything else comes next. Make your decisions that way."

My life on Bedlam Farm has taught me much and helped me a great deal. If you choose to live a life with animals, then you will know death and loss. Farmers love their animals as much as or more than any dog or cat lover, but they keep things in perspective. Farmers birth calves and sheep and goats, knowing these animals will one day be sent away to die. They accept the death of animals in much the same way that animals do—as an integral part of life.

As Maria and I walked through the woods that spring day, I thought about what the farmer from Cossayuna had said. I knew Bartleby had to go. Perspective was a lesson I needed to learn. And learn again.

Perspective isn't something you acquire once and for all. It is a constant struggle, requiring continuous examination, tinkering, and experience. It isn't as if one can draw a clear line and abide by it for good. Animals are living, sentient beings with the power to touch us and evoke and reflect emotion. We know that crates work for dogs. We can't bear to put dogs in crates. We know that dogs need training. We can't bear to discipline them. We know that they don't need people food. We can't stop giving it to them. We know that they don't think in human language. We can't stop putting our thoughts into their heads. Keeping things in perspective is a never-ending process when it comes to living with animals and especially to loving and losing them.

It seems to me that human notions of animals and loss are inadequate. We need a deeper, perhaps more spiritual understanding of animals and their lives and deaths. For centuries, people believed we were superior to animals. In recent years, more and more people seem to be elevating animals, coming to see them as superior to human beings.

I believe that animals such as dogs and cats are not our brothers and sisters, nor are they our children. They are not our underlings, but neither are they our superiors. They live in a different emotional and physical geography than we do. We love them but understand little of their world. They are almost completely dependent on us, yet we have almost none of their great powers of intuition and instinct. They read our emotions with expert ability, yet we know so little of theirs.

By helping Bartleby bond with his mother, by naming him and exploiting him as another cute story on my farm, I lost perspective. Then I regained it. Bartleby became a lamb again. He was not a cute little pet headed for a happy ending on my farm.

Certainly our relationships with dogs and cats are more complex. They have a deeper and more intuitive intelligence than most farm animals. They have been living closely with humans for centuries, and they read us with almost supernatural skill. We open ourselves up to them, trust them, share our homes and our beds with them. Their unconditional love is focused squarely on us, and we need it.

Still, it has been helpful to me to see them as different from human beings. They are not best friends or psychics or empaths or objects of adoration. They deserve our respect as well as our affection.

A farm teaches us the reality of animals and reminds

us of their otherness. On my farm I have seen animals die and killed others. I've put down dogs and shot rabid skunks and raccoons and found the remains of fawns set upon by coyotes. Animals do not live in a no-kill world, and neither do we. Humans and animals are snared by the same net. We will die and so will they. It is perhaps our strongest connection to the animal world, our most universal experience.

A few years before Bartleby came into our lives, I was present for the birth of another lamb. After a long and bloody labor, the newborn went into violent spasms. The vet I called pleaded with me to put the poor thing out of his misery. "But there are all sorts of people around me who would love to take that lamb into their bedrooms and kitchens, bottle-feed him vitamins and milk, diaper and blanket him through the fall and winter months," I told her. Maybe they could save him.

"Please don't do that," the vet urged me. "That is not how animals are meant to live."

Yes, I told her, she was right. I did not wish this ill lamb to be treated like a human baby, transformed into something freakish and unnatural.

I went into the house, loaded up my .22 rifle, and shot the lamb cleanly between the eyes, killing him instantly.

Rose watched quietly as a heavy mist rolled down the

hill and swirled around me. "Thank you," I heard as distinctly as words spoken right into my ear. It might have been a projection. Or a mystical experience. But it rang true to me. Animals deserve the great respect of being treated like animals, not like furry children.

I would not—could not—shoot a dog or a cat. But neither would I unnaturally, expensively, or selfishly prolong its natural life. Perspective is accepting that we are different species, with different rules. It is helpful to me to remember that when a dog or cat I love is dying or dead.

Henry Beston wrote in *The Outermost House* that animals are "other nations, caught with ourselves in the net of life and time, fellow prisoners of the splendour and travail of the earth."

I agree. I am grateful for my time on the farm, for my life among donkeys, dogs, barn cats, cows, steers, goats, chickens, and sheep. They have taught me to accept life and to change with it. They have clarified the notion that my time here is short and that I am in control of very little. They remind me to live in the present, day by day, to be comfortable with myself and accepting of my fate.

I know now that they do not die in the way that we die, terrified and depressed and lamenting their fates. They live in the now, and they die in the same way, and if they can accept their lives and deaths, then so can I.

When the time comes to say goodbye to your pet, whisper to yourself, "Thank you. I let you go and I celebrate your time with us."

One day, Izzy and I were called out to do hospice volunteer work in a small town in the southern tier of the Adirondacks. The hospice coordinator said it was a tough case—a young boy with a brain tumor—and he gave me the opportunity to decline it. But Izzy had been doing hospice therapy for a couple of years, and I was confident about his ability to handle almost anything, even a mission as sensitive as this.

For the next few weeks Izzy and I sat with Jamie. Izzy would come into the house, hop up onto the boy's bed, and lie down. He would find Jamie's hand and nose his head under it. Sometimes Jamie would rub Izzy's head and the two of them would be still for an hour or so, the only sound the respirator helping Jamie to breathe.

At first the boy's exhausted mother would sit on the other side of the bed, stroking Jamie's forehead, as she did day and night. She would read stories to him or sing songs. After a few visits, she saw how calm Jamie was around Izzy. She would lie down on the sofa next to the boy's bed and nap, something she sorely needed to do.

It was during one of these visits that I had a vision— something I had never experienced before. It was shortly before Jamie's death, and the grief and resignation in his mother's face was something I knew I would never forget. Neither would I forget the comfort Izzy brought

Jamie, helping to ease this young boy's journey to the edge of life.

I saw some things so clearly. First, that my love of animals needed to be in proportion to human beings. As I considered how to love animals, and how to mourn and grieve them, I needed to keep Jamie in mind. And the woman down the hill living alone with stomach cancer and little health care or help. The men and women who stagger back from Iraq and Afghanistan with wounds and traumas.

Izzy is connected to all of them, and so am I.

Seeing Izzy with Jamie helped me to understand that our great love for animals works best and most powerfully in proportion to our love for human beings.

Gandhi said that "the greatness of a nation and its moral progress can be judged by the way its animals are treated." That is powerful and true. But then, isn't our progress also defined by the way people are treated? For me, one exists alongside the other, neither in a vacuum.

The glory of animals is in their connection to people, and when I lose that connection, I lose perspective. When I grieve for a dog without thinking of people, I am off balance, and the beautiful human-animal symbiosis is askew.

When an animal of mine dies, I think of Jamie. I think of my sweet grandmother, who loved me so totally. I think of my neighbor who succumbed to cancer. I think of the quiet boy who mowed my lawns and perished in a roadside bomb blast in Iraq.

I think of how we and our animals are, as Henry Beston said, caught in the net of life and time, how they are our fellow travelers.

It is thinking of people that puts the death of animals in a proper and rational light. Jamie taught me to be mindful of people when I mourn animals. Izzy taught me to be mindful of both. For me, that is true perspective, solid ground on which to walk. It's important and healthy to differentiate between grieving for people and grieving for animals. I embrace the Quaker ideal: human life is sacred. Animal life is precious. In understanding the difference between the two, I have found a way to grieve that is comfortable for me.

A friend of mine told me that she loved her cats because they were so smart, and most of the people she knew were so dumb. Another said that he mourned his Lab because he was so nice and people were so cruel.

I told them I was sorry to hear it. I do not love animals at the expense of people. Animals have not taught me that people are dumb or cruel or hopeless. Animals have kept love alive in me; they have been my bridge to people, my path to humanity. I think our humanity is defined by the way we love animals and the way they love us.

How can you keep things in perspective?

My suggestion is this: when animals die, think not

only of them but also of the people they touched. Of the love and laughter and comfort and companionship they brought to people. Think of the people you knew and loved who have left the world.

Sometimes we humans forget how to connect to one another. Dogs and cats never forget how to connect to us. Animals have taught me how to love purely. And patiently. They have helped fill some of the lonely gaps of life. They have helped me to be a better human being. That, I think, is their legacy and glorious purpose.

If you honor this legacy, it will bring you perspective and help to heal your broken heart.

Helping Children

KIDS ARE THE PUREST ANIMAL lovers in the world. Psychologists have long noted the power of animal friendships and fantasies in the development of children. So there are special challenges in talking to children about the death of a family pet. Too many well-intentioned parents take the easy way out when dealing with this issue. But lying to kids is never the answer.

Like a lot of kids, Allie was sharp and prided herself on knowing what was going on in her family. She was a loner, an observer. She was good at piecing together bits of information—feelings, looks, whispers, and snatches of adult conversations. If she rarely knew exactly what was going on, she always knew when *something* was.

Allie was nine when she came home from school one hot afternoon, looking around, as she always did, for Otis, the sweet old yellow Lab who had been such an important part of every single day of her life.

Allie played with Otis in the yard, slept with him at night, kissed him on the nose, scratched his belly, told him secrets, and listened to his. She had thrown him a zillion balls, brought him on sleepovers, laughed—and secretly cheered him on—when he stole food off the kitchen counter. They stayed warm together on cold winter nights, and every morning, she woke up to Otis's gentle licks and nuzzles on her cheek.

Allie even went to the vet with Otis to help him feel safe, and to soothe him when he trembled and tried to run and hide. Now, as an adult looking back, Allie believes Otis taught her how to live and how to trust. She loved him to death and could not imagine life without him.

That afternoon, when she walked in the door, all of her senses told her right away that something was wrong.

Her mother looked awful, her father looked sad, out of it. And Otis wasn't there to greet her.

"Where's Otis?" she asked. Her father cleared his throat, mumbled something about work and picked up the phone. Her mother went into the kitchen, saying she'd be back shortly. Allie ran upstairs. Otis's bed was empty. She looked out the window. He wasn't in the backyard. She ran back downstairs and repeatedly pressed her mother.

"Oh, sweetie . . . Otis is sick. He's in the hospital." Her mother looked away.

"Will he be all right?"

"I'm sure he'll be fine. Let's talk about your day."

Allie didn't want to talk about her day. She found her father. He said Otis was sick and might not be home for a while.

Allie accepted this state of affairs for the first few days, then demanded more and more angrily to know where Otis was, why she couldn't see him, why he wasn't home. Her parents had trouble looking at her, talking to her. They always pretended to be busy.

Months later, her mother told Allie that Otis was dead, and had gone off to a dog farm in the sky. They hadn't wanted to upset her, her parents said, because they knew how much Otis had meant to her.

Allie still recalls the shock of losing Otis, and her confusion and anger at her parents, her fury at their lies. She came to understand that her parents were only trying to protect her, but she harbored angry feelings for a long time. Many years later, she sat down with her mother, who told her that she'd avoided the truth because Allie had been too young to handle Otis's death. Allie tried to make her mother understand that what she had trouble handling was being lied to. She had always known that Otis was dead, she said, from the second she walked into the house. If only they had told the truth, if only they had respected her enough to be honest, she wouldn't still be trying to find peace and closure decades later.

Allie has vowed that if her daughter ever comes home to find her dog missing, she will sit down with her right away and tell her what happened. She will show her child that she trusts her enough to deal with loss. She would always be sure her daughter had the chance to say goodbye to her pet. Because there is a little piece of Allie that will never forgive her parents for not letting her say goodbye to Otis—a tiny grief that so far has not let her go.

It is simple, even natural, to patronize children, to protect and exclude them from the reality of the world or to conclude that they don't have much to contribute to the process of overcoming grief and loss.

William learned otherwise. "I was showing photos of my dogs to my friend's four-year-old son. I told him I had two dogs, yet there were three in the picture. He asked me why. At first, I thought that I shouldn't tell him what had happened. Then I decided to be honest with him, to just tell him that my dog had died. He said, 'I'm really sorry that your dog died, but I'm glad your wife has someone to keep her company in heaven.'

"My wife had died a few months earlier. This was the sweetest thing anyone could have said. The boy wasn't crying, but I was, and he came over to comfort me. Here I was worrying about upsetting him, and he ends up consoling me."

As William came to understand, it's a mistake to underestimate children. They have eyes and ears and access to all kinds of knowledge, especially in the information age. They know about life and loss, and, within reason, psychologists believe it's important to give them the chance to deal with difficult aspects of the human experience.

There is no universal advice encompassing all kids when it comes to grieving for animals. Each child has different needs and methods of coping. Anthea's story demonstrates a mother really listening to her child and taking responsible steps to help her deal with the death of a beloved pet.

Anthea's eight-year-old daughter, Samantha, had grown up with and was deeply attached to their rescue dog, Charlotta. Now Charlotta had liver cancer and the time was fast approaching when she would need to be euthanized in order to spare her suffering. Anthea began to prepare her daughter for the loss she knew was coming. She showed Samantha Charlotta's X-rays and let her help give the dog her medicine. On the day that Charlotta was to be put down, Samantha asked if she could come along. Anthea hesitated, and called the school psychologist for advice. The psychologist suggested that Samantha drive with her mom and Charlotta to the vet, but say goodbye to the dog in the waiting room. Anthea followed this plan, then left Samantha with the receptionist while she and Charlotta went in to see the vet. When it was over, Samantha came in to see the dog and say another round of goodbyes. "She was a part of it, but didn't have to witness it. It was a good decision for her," says Anthea.

Donna needed to take an entirely different approach with her son, Derek, who she describes as "a bit of an engineer." Derek loves computers and software, and Donna framed their conversation about the death of the family dog in terms she felt he could most relate to. "I told him that everything has an average design life in this world, and when something—human, animal, car, or computer— reaches the end of its design life, it ceases to function. This is normal and happens to everyone and everything. It's okay to miss the dog and be sad, I told him, but animals dying is a fact of life."

Donna concedes that this is a non-emotional approach to managing grief, but she also believes it worked for her son. Her story underscores that all kids are different and parents need to tailor their techniques to fit the individual child. I might find Donna's approach a tad cold, but for Derek, the idea of his dog's "design life" helped him understand and accept his loss.

Including older children in end-of-life decisions for animals can help them deal with the impending loss in a healthy manner. Kids love their pets and are entitled to be involved in the process.

Sara held a family meeting when their eight-year-old rabbit was near death. She and her two children went over the options. When she explained that Bummer was suffering, the family agreed unanimously to let the rabbit die a natural death, without medication or surgery.

"I told the kids that it was my decision, not theirs; my responsibility and not theirs. But that I really wanted to hear what they thought. And I did. They all fought to keep Bummer alive if possible, but gradually accepted the reality. Children are durable, tougher than people give them credit for. Many parents try to solve all the problems of the world for their kids. I want them to learn how to handle problems intelligently and compassionately."

Parents have many tools to help them share the grieving process with their children. Families can create photo albums and save them online, or in blogs and social media sites. Low-tech options include drawing, painting, and journaling together during an animal's last weeks. I know one mother who had the family dog's photo reproduced on a blanket weeks before he died, and her daughter slept with it for months. New graphic and computing software and programs make it easy and inexpensive to write and print (both on paper and online) books with photos, poems, songs, stories, and words commemorating a family's life with a pet. Many I have seen are beautiful and healing. Creating these books is something productive and tangible that parents can do with children, and that families can do together. Kids often return to them, until some of their loss has faded.

I helped one family write a prayer for their nine-year-old cat, Betty, after she was struck and killed by a speeding truck. The two children in the family—ages six and nine—read it aloud before bedtime for several weeks after Betty was killed.

Dear God,
Please welcome Betty into her new home.
She was good to us, and she loved us,
and we loved her back.
We are grateful for her presence
in our home. For her loving us and
protecting us and sharing our lives.
For growing up with us.
We know that animals like Betty do not live as long
as we do.
We give thanks for her, and we miss her,
but we hope she is running and playing and

chasing after mice and squirrels in her new home.
And sitting by a warm fire when it gets chilly.
We send her kisses and hugs.

The simple act of reciting this prayer seemed to help the children. It allowed them to acknowledge their sadness, focus on gratitude rather than loss, and imagine their cat in a peaceful and safe place.

For families dealing with the death of a pet, it's important for parents to share the experience of grief with their kids, rather than ignore it or simply wait for it to pass. Acknowledging loss is important. Children's grief ought not to be rushed or diminished any more than the pain adults feel when their animals die.

Here are some ways to honor your child's experience during this difficult time:

1. When a dog or cat comes into the home, consider talking briefly, gently, about loss. Explain to your children that animals don't live as long as people; that several dogs and cats might come into the life of the family over time.
2. If a pet dies suddenly, include the children. Help them share happy memories of the dog or cat. Have them write poems or paint pictures, share photographs and stories. Join with them in planning a memorial service, or building a monument to the dog or cat.

3. If a pet is ill, let the children know as soon as possible. Show them the animal's medications. If the vet permits, bring them to the animal hospital, let them see what happens there, where their dog or cat might go.

4. Change the scene. A surprising number of parents tell me that when a dog, cat or other pet dies, they take their children for a drive. "These days," says Susie, "you need to get them into a car. It's the only place where you can limit distractions. Kids talk in cars, and they listen there. When our dog died, I took the kids for a ride. We cried, laughed, got burgers, and got through."

It's important to stress that there are many different approaches to dealing with kids and grief, and that if grieving goes on for weeks or months, and is intense or otherwise alarming, it is best to seek professional help.

Psychologists have long believed that powerful realities like death, grief, and loss are opportunities to teach children how to grow and learn and live in the world. I saw that very clearly when I visited two elementary school classes in Upstate New York—one in Saratoga Springs and the other in Washington County—to read from my first children's book, *Meet the Dogs of Bedlam Farm*.

The two districts were very different demographically—

Saratoga Springs is an affluent city teeming with horse people and expensive condos, and Washington County, where my farm is, is a poor and mostly rural farming community.

Despite these differences, the third and fourth graders I was reading to had the following things in common: a love of animals, and many stories about losing them. With parents and teachers present, our discussions veered toward the loss of pets.

Jill told me she once had a pet hamster, but it had been stalked and eaten by her cat. She said she loved both the hamster and the cat very much, but she was angry at the cat after it killed her hamster.

"Was it hard?" I asked her.

She shrugged and nodded yes.

"How do you feel about it now?"

Jill said that her Mom told her that cats were wonderful, but even though they were cute, it was their nature to hunt and kill small animals like hamsters. The cat didn't mean any harm; she was just doing what cats do. Jill got another hamster, but it got sick and died. The cat is still in her house, Jill said, and sleeps on her bed, which makes her very happy.

When Lucas's golden retriever died, he emailed a picture of the dog to his cousin Andrew in Colorado, and Andrew sent him a picture of his dog who had died too. This made him feel better. He said he knows that dogs and cats die, and you are sad, but then you try and get another one. His parents told him they would let him get another dog soon, and he couldn't wait.

Sandy said when her dog, Timber, died, she and her parents dug a big hole in their backyard and her dad buried the dog with his biscuits and toys out by the garden. She put a drawing of Timber on the grave, and her dad told her that when she got sad, she should go out to the grave and say a prayer for Timber, and pray that he was well and chasing his ball in heaven, and so that's what she did.

Ron lives on a farm. He's seen many animals die. He talks about cows that got sick or were sent away, cats taken by foxes and coyotes, dogs run over on the highway. Yes, it makes him sad sometimes, he said. But there were a lot of animals in the world and his mom said they teach us to use our time well and be grateful for it.

Parents instinctively look for tools to help their children when they've suffered the loss of a pet. Therapists, books, blogs, and online support groups can all be excellent sources of assistance for families grieving for their animals. But I've often sensed in the stories children tell me that the sensitivity, support, and thoughtfulness of good parents means the most to them.

Marissa, a farm mother, is one of those parents.

"It was very hard on her," said Marissa, whose seven-year-old daughter had just lost her pet chicken, Gertrude.

"She took that chicken everywhere, walked her on a leash, marched with her in town parades, slept alongside of her. (Gertrude slept in a cage.) Lord, she so loved that bird. But we sat down with her, and we talked to her and helped her understand that chickens aren't the heartiest of pets. We had done all we could to save Gertrude. Pets come into our lives, we told her, and we can't stop loving with that one animal. There is so much love to give and so many animals that depend on us humans to love and care for them.

"It's a different kind of loss when your child goes through it," Marissa continued. "Very tough, and you have to be prepared for it. I told my daughter if we want to love again, this is the ultimate price we pay. We have other chickens, so my daughter knew the love wouldn't stop with Gertrude's death. Now we share the great stories we have with Roger (who we thought was a rooster at first, but the name stuck). Death is a part of life, my daughter now understands. It will happen, guaranteed, but we can't stop caring. And she says she learned so much from that. I can see that she did. I guess anything can be a blessing."

Kids cannot escape the overpowering reality of life and death any more than adults can. Friends, relatives, grandparents can get sick and die, or suffer in accidents and tragedies. The loss of pets can be a window for children into the profound, and inevitable, experiences life has in store for all of us.

It is sad to lose a pet. But for children as well as adults, that is not the only thing it needs to be. As children testify in their own voices and words, they don't live in bubbles, much as we wish they did. Their—our—lives are as shaped and defined by pain and loss as they are by love and happiness.

And the loss of a dog or cat or hamster or chicken can teach kids something about all of those things.

Getting
Another Pet

AFTER A PET DIES, NOTHING IS MORE healing than experiencing that kind of relationship again. All of my dogs have been so wonderful—so loving and uplifting—that I have paid them the high compliment of going out and getting another dog soon after their death.

I adhere to few rules, but one of them is this: people who love dogs and cats should have them.

There are many millions of dogs and cats languishing in cages in shelters who would be pleased to come and love people who have lost their beloved pets. It's easy to find one, and inexpensive, and satisfying beyond words.

There is a dog or cat for everybody. An eighty-year-old neighbor was devastated when she lost her cat, but she told me that she was too old to get another pet—it wouldn't be fair. We went to a shelter near Glens Falls, New York, and found a fourteen-year-old cat whose owners had died. She only had a year or two left to live and was very happy to spend her remaining days in my neighbor's lap. People say they're too busy to get another dog, but many older dogs would be only too happy to get out of their crates in their shelters and spend their last days napping in the living rooms of busy people who are out at work.

I hope that one day you will be able to get another dog or cat and love it as much as you loved this one. Some people aren't ready for that. They think it's disloyal, or they haven't worked through their guilt, or they feel they simply can't bear to go through the grief of losing an animal again. That, to me, is the saddest outcome, for people and for the millions of dogs and cats in search of a loving home.

When my friend Julie called to talk about getting a new dog, I knew better than to push. I have a reputation for successfully matching people and dogs, but I could tell that Julie was still grieving for Streak, her greyhound rescue, even after nearly three years. Julie and Streak had had an exceptionally close bond. She had saved the greyhound from a South Carolina racetrack hours before the dog was scheduled to be put down for a bad leg. She had healed Streak and Streak had healed her. (Julie was then fresh from a bad divorce and the collapse of a company she had helped start.) Over the course of nine years, they had "built a new life together." But, as happens with pets, Streak died first.

On the phone, Julie talked about her mixed feelings. She was reluctant to get another dog, but she also missed having one very much. I agreed to help and told her we could take it slow.

I pegged Julie as a Lab person. A jogger, hiker, and camper, she loves to go out into the woods and mountains for days and weeks at a stretch. So I introduced her to Samantha, a wonderful Lab breeder in Saratoga Springs, New York. They talked by email, then by phone, and finally Julie made a trip to the kennel to see the dogs and learn about the breed.

Samantha introduced her to a sweet, pregnant yellow Lab. She also met the sire, a genial black Lab. Julie went home still feeling ambivalent, but for all her reservations, when Samantha called to say that the Lab was in labor, Julie hopped into her Subaru and drove to Saratoga. She sat up with Samantha all night helping with the birth.

In truth, Julie did not find the newborn pups appealing. They were tiny, rodentlike with their eyes closed. What was there to love? But when she came back a month later, the puppies' eyes were open and their individual personalities were starting to show. Julie was drawn to a yellow female, who kept looking at her and wagging her tail, but she did not feel certain enough—or confident enough—to make a decision just yet.

A few weeks later, Samantha called her up.

"You know that dog you've been eyeing?"

Julie was startled. Had she been that obvious?

"I think she's the dog for you. Come see for yourself."

Samantha says it often happens that a dog and a human choose each other. And that's what happened with Julie and the puppy she would name Melody.

When Julie got to Samantha's, Melody seemed to be expecting her. "It was as if she had her bags packed and was looking out the window waiting for me." As soon as Julie picked her up, Melody curled up on her shoulder, licking her chin and sighing with pleasure. Julie's heart filled with joy.

I have seen it over and over again. When people are ready, the spirit of a dog can wash away an astonishing amount of pain and loss.

Later that week, Julie sent me this email:

"Jon, thanks for not pushing me to get a dog before I was ready, but for reminding me that there are other dogs in the world, and they would love a home. Melody and I connected in the most amazing way. When she looked up at me, I just felt her saying, 'I am your dog, and you are my human,' and it was one of the sweetest and most touching moments of my life."

Julie would later tell me that one night she went out into the backyard and hung Streak's collar off of a low-hanging tree branch. It was time, she thought, to move on. She could see how much she would love Melody and how much Melody would love her.

She felt some pangs about Streak, a fear of abandoning her and her memory.

"But then," she said, "I closed my eyes, and I imagined Streak running across the field, loping like a gazelle in that way of hers, and then turning to me and smiling, and saying, 'Good for you, Julie, good for you.' She was cheering me on. And then she just sailed off out of sight."

When a pet dies, we do have choices, and this has always made me feel better. We can grieve as long and as deeply as we wish or need to. If there is anything positive that comes out of the loss of a pet, it might be this: there are so many more waiting for you.

The choice is yours.

Letter from
a Dog

I DON'T GENERALLY BELIEVE IN
ghosts, but the spirits of my dogs
who've died haunt me all the time.

I see Orson on the porch, staring
into the valley, as he loved to do.

I see Julius and Stanley curled up in
the basement of my home in New Jer-

sey, snoring contentedly as I struggled to put together a writing life.

I see Clarence lying on the foot of my daughter's bed when she was so small, her feet resting on his back.

My friend Lesley, the shaman and animal communicator, says my dogs come by to check up on me, then move along. Sometimes when I feel the wind stroking my cheek or a special warmth in my soul, I see them and feel them. I say hello.

And I say goodbye. I think of the things I wish I had told them.

I think of the things they might have wished to tell me.

If our dogs could leave us with final thoughts, here's what I imagine their parting words might be:

Dear Friend,
It is my time to say goodbye. My legs are weakening, my sight failing, smells are faint. I am wearying. My spirit is fading, and I have been called home and away from you.

I wish to be strong again, to roll in gross stuff, to snatch greasy bones, to eat all of the things you hated me to eat, to have my belly scratched for all time, to run through the fields and the woods, to smell the stories of life, and to raise my nose to the wind and see the world all over again.

I am going home. I know I leave you in loneliness and pain. That is the way of people when they say goodbye. Dogs are different. We don't have regrets or wish that we could alter the story of life.

Although I have been called away, I leave you with the memories of our life together.

I remember a cold winter's night when you sang to me in the dark as the wind howled and snow drifted outside the window. I felt your loneliness and knew my work.

When you looked at me and the corners of your mouth turned up, you smelled and looked different. Lighter, happier. That was my life, my work. Nothing more clearly defined my purpose. When you smiled, I knew why I was here.

I never tired of watching you, of being with you while you lived your life. I sat by your side, entering into the spirit of the moment. I supported your life, wherever it went, whatever you felt, whatever you did. I was your witness, your testament.

I remember walking in the snow. And running alongside you. And chasing after balls, Frisbees, sticks. And warm fires on cold nights. And sitting by you when you read books or watched baseball games.

I remember my heart jumping out of my chest when you came home and called my name, or grabbed a ball, or took me outside, or fed me. I hope you know that I loved all of those things—

whatever you chose to bring me and give me, whatever time you spent with me, I loved.

And I thank you.

I always knew where you were, even when you forgot me or couldn't see me. You had no secrets from me. You showed me everything. We trusted each other.

Unlike people, I would never hurt you. I could never hurt you. It is not an instinct I possess.

I smelled and felt all of the worries in a human life, but I am different. Like other animals, I want only what I need. Your life is too complex for me to grasp. There are so many things in it that are meaningless to me.

I am so much simpler than you.

I love you and I love all the people and animals in our home. And I love food and smelly things in the woods and balls and Frisbees and bones. There is not much more to me than that, and yet you loved me for it, and despite it.

By now, you must know that there is always a goodbye hovering in the shadow of a dog. We are never here for long, or for long enough. We were never meant to share all of your life, only to mark its passages. We come and we go. We come when we are needed. We leave when it is time. Death is necessary. It defines life.

I will see you again.

I will watch over you.

I hope, in your grief and loneliness, that you will consider how sad it would have been had we not had this time together, not had the chance to give each other so much.

I do not mourn or grieve, but I will miss standing beside you, bound together on our walk through life, even as I know that there is a long line of others waiting to take my place and stand with you.

Thank you. It was nothing but a gift.

And finally, I ask these things of you:

Remember me.

Celebrate me.

Grieve for me.

And then, when you can, let me go, freely and in peace.

When you are ready, do me the great honor of bringing another dog into your life, so you can give and receive this gift again.

Afterword

by Debra A. Katz, M.D.

ANIMALS PLAY COMPLICATED AND central roles in our lives. In our often harried and disconnected world, our pets anchor us, connect us with others, and provide a kind of emotional sustenance that is different from what we get from people. It frequently comes as a surprise, however, that we react so strongly to their deaths.

Why does the loss of our pets affect us so much? This is a complicated question, and the answer is different for each person. The death of a pet is harder for some of us than for others. In spite of comments we might hear, such as "She's just a dog" or "He's only a cat," our relationships with pets constitute important attachments in our lives. Animals silently share in our most significant as well as our most mundane experiences. They allow us to express feelings that we often don't show to the rest of the world and provide a physical comfort and contact that is different from any other we experience on a daily basis. We wonder about what our pets think and how they feel about us. Because we can't use language to communicate, we make up all kinds of stories about what goes on in their heads. There remains a certain unknowability and mystery around what happens in the minds of animals, which accentuates their "otherness" but can also serve to enhance the range of feelings we can access with them. Our interactions with our pets might end up revealing as much—if not more—about us as about them.

As a psychiatrist and psychoanalyst, I spend a lot of time thinking and talking about relationships, what drives them, what causes trouble, how people feel in them and what happens when they end. Our understanding of what we experience when a pet dies is based on the kind of attachment we have to that animal in life as well as on some of the unique qualities of interspecies connections. Dogs and cats function as attachment objects, similar in some ways to our relationships with infants or young children because of the intimacy and sensuality of touching, petting, and holding them, the speechless communication that takes place as we read each other's behavior and intentions, and the way they allow us to play and be silly. Although we like to think of ourselves as attachment figures for our pets, our pets might, in fact, function in more important ways as attachment figures for us.

An attachment figure is someone who provides a sense of security, comfort, and protection, who is sought out at times of distress, and who allows exploration of the world and expression of a wide range of feelings. The infant-parent relationship is the earliest attachment relationship, with the infant seeking to remain close to the parent and expressing distress when separation or loss is threatened. Infants, however, grow into children, who develop speech, tell us what they think (sometimes to our dismay), grow and change dramatically over time, and eventually become adults and leave home. Animals don't change the way children do; they never talk, and they seem perpetually young and dependent, so their deaths almost always feel premature.

As attachment figures, pets often evoke feelings from our earliest relationships, providing a closeness and security that is quite powerful. It makes sense that when this relationship is disrupted, the resulting loss provokes strong reactions. The sense of responsibility for a creature who is dependent on us for survival and for whom we make decisions regarding life and death adds a dimension that is different than in human relationships. The fact that we can't talk to or know what our pets are thinking or feeling, how much pain or discomfort they are in, what they would want if they could make their choices known, and what will happen in the future intensifies our sense of responsibility and guilt over these decisions.

Thinking rationally about decisions regarding euthanasia or the cost involved in keeping a pet alive becomes entangled with worries about how our pets will feel about having their lives cut short, how much they will miss us, and what separation and death means to them. These decisions are wrenching and filled with ambivalence, and as Jon Katz points out, they are often not considered in advance or in any kind of organized fashion. This book provides a way to think about these issues before we are required to act on behalf of a gravely ill animal. It helps us understand that what we feel about deciding it is time to end our pets' suffering is very different from what our animals feel toward us.

There is much to be learned from making end-of-life decisions for our animals. Our worries about what our pet is experiencing tell us something about ourselves. For example, we may wonder, "Will she hold it against me?" "Did she know I loved her?" "Will she know I tried to do everything I could?" These are universal questions that reflect something about the wordless and powerful nature of our relationships with animals but might also reveal something specific about our own, often unarticulated, anxieties. Did we hold it against someone who did not prepare us for a loss early in our lives? Did we tell the people we loved and who are now gone that we loved them? Do we feel resentful toward family members who didn't do everything they could in the face of loss or death? These questions and uncomfortable feelings, long suppressed, can surface when a beloved animal faces illness and death.

Mourning the death of a pet is different from mourning the death of a person. Our relationships with pets are mostly private, and may not be recognized or may be minimized by others. There are no socially sanctioned mourning rituals for this type of loss. Mourning is a necessary process that allows us to come to terms with the fact that our pet has died and that we will never see him again. It hurts and is sad, but by allowing ourselves to grieve, we come closer to accepting that our pet is gone. Although we recognize intellectually that we will never see our pet again, it is much harder to accept this emotionally. This accounts for experiences such as hearing our pet's tags jingling, feeling her leaning against our leg, or expecting to see her sleeping in her favorite spot. These common experiences remind us that it takes time to accept the death of a pet we have loved. Feelings of sadness and longing for our pet catch us off guard, come at odd moments, and remind us that mourning a pet is not something that can be planned or organized. It proceeds at its own pace and can last for a short or a very long time, depending on how intense our attachment was to our pet and what he or she meant to us.

For many people, the loss of a pet is a uniquely private and painful experience and deprives them of something that might be hard to attain in human relationships—a bond that is pure and associated with a sense of unconditional love. There is no easy way around loss and grief, but accepting our sadness, acknowledging the irreplaceability of our pet, and trying to share our feelings with trusted others might help. We often do not want to burden others with our feelings, but talking about our pain and sharing memories of our pet allows us to put into words—sometimes for the first time—what we have lost and helps connect us to others who understand. Telling stories about our pet allows us to get in touch with the funny, tender, and exasperating moments that are part of living with an animal. Sharing these with others or reminiscing quietly to ourselves simultaneously helps preserve these memories and helps us let go.

When feelings of loss and grief seem to be too intense or overwhelming, persist for too long a time, or interfere with our functioning, talking with a professional might help. Difficulty with mourning a pet might be a sign that we need to attend to other experiences of loss in our lives or that our relationship to our pet is complicated in ways we might need help to understand.

The loss of a pet affects not only individuals but families too. Pets are family members in their own right and reveal much about the family in terms of their role, who is considered their "favorite," the feelings and intentions that are projected onto them, the stories told about them, the names they are called, and the behavioral problems they experience. Children identify with pets as vulnerable, dependent creatures. They share confidences with the pet about sensitive issues and learn about the facts of life and death through their pets. The death of a cherished dog or cat is often a child's introduction to loss and allows the child to see how feelings of sadness are dealt with in the family. Children learn what is acceptable to express and what isn't and what religious beliefs and rituals surround death.

Knowing that a dog or cat is about to die or will need to be put to sleep provides an opportunity to discuss death and shows a child that he can rely on his parent to prepare him for a difficult experience. If a pet is very old or ill, initiating a discussion about death allows the child to begin to prepare and creates an atmosphere of trust in the parent for future questions or anxieties. While not all deaths can be prepared for, involving children in conversations about euthanasia helps them not feel caught by surprise. Pets often provide children with their first experience with responsibility and caretaking, so including children in discussions about a pet's impending death recognizes their importance in the life of the pet. It also gives them time to come to terms with what's happening and allows them to make choices about their participation in the process.

Gearing explanations to the age of the child, being clear that death is permanent, avoiding confusing language such as "being put to sleep," helping the child understand what actually happens when a pet is euthanized or dies a natural death, and talking about what will happen afterward in terms of burial or cremation all give children information and a context to understand what is happening. It also enhances confidence that the parent is not afraid to discuss these painful realities. For parents, it might feel cruel to expose children to sadness and death and demonstrate our helplessness to protect them. But avoiding these conversations confirms children's fears that these experiences are too painful or anxiety-provoking to discuss and must be managed alone. Children want to be involved with the death of their pets and look to their parents to lead the way.

The death of a pet may facilitate conversations about larger issues such as the unfairness of life, the lack of safety or predictability in the world, and how to go on in the face of what feels like unbearable loss. How parents behave—not just what they say—provides a kind of modeling for how emotionally intense experiences are handled in a family. When we allow our children to see us feel sad or admit to missing the pet, we teach them that death can be talked about and that painful feelings don't need to be hidden.

While there is no specific timetable for getting a new pet, it is important to consider the motivation carefully. Are we trying to help our children bypass grief, or are we ready to reinvest our love in a new animal? Allowing ourselves and our children time to mourn, talking about what the pet meant to the family, and sharing our grief provide ways of honoring relationships—with the pet and with one another. They introduce children to the idea that relationships are important and shouldn't be taken for granted and that when they end, there is a way of bearing what might seem to be unbearable with the support of others. These are not lessons that can be taught or provided to children in an intellectual way; rather they come from experiencing the loss of a beloved pet with family members who can allow the child to feel, talk about, and learn from their grief.

This book encourages the reader to welcome grief and to honor it as a sign of the depth of our feeling for pets we have loved. At the same time, it challenges us to think about the place of pets in our lives and the problems that arise, for both humans and animals, when we try to get too many of our emotional needs met through them. Our struggle to keep our relationships with pets in perspective is a natural outcome of the kinds of primal feelings they evoke in us that connect with our earliest emotional experiences. This adds to the complexity of the grief we feel when we lose a pet. Current losses inevitably remind us of past losses and in this way the loss of a pet can serve as an opportunity to revisit or rework earlier losses. We are often not aware of this while it's happening and discover, as we long for a pet who recently died, that the feelings this loss evokes are very similar to what we experienced when a close relative or friend died or when we find that someone from our past is on our mind in new ways. It used to be thought that the work of mourning was to break psychological ties with a lost relationship in order to reinvest fully in a new relationship. We now know that mourning involves finding some way of remaining connected internally with our loved ones in order to find a place for them in our current lives. With our pets, this might simply be through the act of remembering or quietly thinking about them, through sharing stories about them or honoring them in some official way. When we are able to do this, we preserve the emotional gifts we've received from those extraordinary animals.

About the Author

JON KATZ has written twenty books—seven novels and thirteen works of nonfiction—including *Soul of a Dog, Izzy & Lenore, Dog Days, A Good Dog,* and *The Dogs of Bedlam Farm.* He has written for *The New York Times, The Wall Street Journal,* Slate, *Rolling Stone,* and the *AKC Gazette.* He has worked for CBS News, the *Boston Globe, The Washington Post,* and *The Philadelphia Inquirer.* Katz is also a photographer and the author of a children's book, *Meet the Dogs of Bedlam Farm.* He lives on Bedlam Farm in Upstate New York with his wife, the artist Maria Wulf; his dogs, Rose, Izzy, Lenore, and Frieda; his donkeys, Lulu and Fanny; and his barn cats, Mother and Minnie.

About the Type

This book was set in Granjon, a modern re-cutting of a typeface produced under the direction of George W. Jones, who based Granjon's design upon the letter forms of Claude Garamond (1480–1561). The name was given to the typeface as a tribute to the typographic designer Robert Granjon.

tortured "cheetah and gazelle" negotiations and so on—the sudden outbreak of hostility seemed shocking. "I think everyone thought they were witnessing a knife fight," Sloan Harris, codirector of the literary department at International Creative Management, said at the time. "And it looks like we've gone to the nukes."[17]

A few days later, under a barrage of criticism for making authors and customers collateral damage in the fight, Amazon relented. Bezos and his Kindle team collaborated on a public message, which they posted on an Amazon online forum: "We have expressed our strong disagreement and the seriousness of our disagreement by temporarily ceasing the sale of all Macmillan titles. We want you to know that ultimately, however, we will have to capitulate and accept Macmillan's terms because Macmillan has a monopoly over their own titles, and we will want to offer them to you even at prices we believe are needlessly high for e-books....Kindle is a business for Amazon, and it is also a mission. We never expected it to be easy!"

Ironically, the shift to the agency model made the Kindle business more profitable, since Amazon was forced to charge more for e-books, and Amazon held a near monopoly on e-book sales. That helped Amazon sustain the gradual decrease in the price of the Kindle hardware. Less than two years later, the cheapest Kindle e-reader would cost seventy-nine dollars.

But Amazon wasn't sitting back or letting others dictate the own terms. Over the next year, Amazon responded forcefully several ways. Russ Grandinetti, who had moved over to Kin from apparel, and David Naggar, the new hire from Ran House, made the rounds of midsize publishers like Houghton flin. According to several executives at those firms, they warned that they did not have the leverage to move to an pricing model and that Amazon would stop selling their b they did. Amazon also intensified its focus on its own publishing business, which would cause another wave of dis publishers in the years ahead.

In trying to loosen Amazon's grip on the e-book market lishers and Apple created a significant new problem for t

A day after the standoff with Macmillan, according to court documents, Amazon sent a white paper to the Federal Trade Commission and the U.S. Department of Justice laying out the chain of events and its suspicion that the publishers and Apple were engaged in an illegal conspiracy to fix e-book prices.

Many publishing executives suspect that Amazon played a major role in provoking the legal brouhaha that resulted. But antitrust investigators likely didn't need much nudging. Incredibly, even though Steve Jobs passed away in the fall of 2011, his earlier comments dug the legal hole deeper for Apple and the five agency publishers. In the biography *Steve Jobs,* Walter Isaacson quoted Jobs as saying, "Amazon screwed it up…Before Apple even got on the scene, some booksellers were starting to withhold books from Amazon. So we told the publishers, 'We'll go to the agency model, where set the price, and we get our 30%, and yes, the customer pays a more, but that's what you want anyway.'"

's patronizing statement was potentially incriminating. If
rs had engaged in a joint effort to make customers pay "a
e," that was the foundation on which antitrust cases were
Justice Department sued Apple and the five publishers
, 2012, accusing them of illegally conspiring to raise
s. All the publishers eventually settled without admit-
while Apple alone held out, claiming that it had done
g and that its intent was only to expand the market for

gainst Apple was heard the following June in a Man-
om and lasted for seventeen days. District judge
en found Apple liable, ruling that it had conspired
publishers to eliminate price competition and raise
nd had therefore violated Section 1 of the Sherman
Apple vowed to appeal the verdict. A hearing on
nding at the time this book went to press.
ttle played out publicly in both the courtroom and
a But despite the case's visibility in the media, it was
arger rise of Amazon at the time, an ascent inter-

rupted by the great recession that resumed with renewed vigor afterward.

Beginning in 2009, as the fog of the economic crisis lifted, Amazon's quarterly growth rate returned to its pre-recession levels, and over the next two years, the stock climbed 236 percent. The world was broadly recognizing Amazon's potential — the power of Prime and of Amazon's mighty fulfillment network, the promise of AWS, and the steady gains seen in Asia and Europe. In part because of the e-book pricing war, investors began to understand that the Kindle could grab an outsize share of the book business and that the device had the potential to do to bookstores what iTunes had done to record shops. Analysts en masse upgraded their ratings on Amazon's stock, and mutual fund managers added the company to their portfolios. For the first time, *Amazon* was spoken in the same breath as *Google* and *Apple* — not as an afterthought, but as an equal. It had blasted off into high orbit.

CHAPTER 10

Expedient Convictions

The spectacular rise of Amazon's visibility and market power in the wake of the great recession brought the company more frequently into the public eye, but the attention was not always flattering. During the years 2010 and 2011, the company battled a growing chorus of critics over its avoidance of collecting state sales tax, the mechanics behind two of its large acquisitions, its move into the business of publishing books (in competition with its own suppliers), and what appeared to be its systematic disregard for the pricing policies of major manufacturers. Almost overnight, the company that viewed itself as the perennial underdog now seemed to many like a remote and often arrogant giant who was trying to play by his own set of rules.

Bezos (and the few Jeff Bots that Amazon allowed to speak in public) perfected an attitude of bemused perplexity when addressing criticisms. Bezos often said that Amazon had a "willingness to be misunderstood," which was an impressive piece of rhetorical jujitsu — the implication being that its opponents just didn't *understand* the company.[1] Bezos also deflected attacks by claiming that Amazon was a missionary company, not a mercenary one. That dichotomy originated with now former board member John Doerr, who formulated it after reading his partner Randy Komisar's 2001 business-philosophy book *The Monk and the Riddle*. Missionaries have righteous goals and are trying to make the world a better place. Mercenaries are out for money and power and will run over anyone who gets in the way. To Bezos, at least, there was no doubt where Amazon fell. "I would take a missionary over a mercenary any day," he liked to say. "One of those great paradoxes is that it's usually the missionaries who end up making more money anyway."[2]

Amazon spokespeople approached these controversies with simple, direct points that they repeated over and over, rarely veering into the uncomfortable details of the company's aggressive tactics. The arguments had the advantage of being completely rational while also serving Amazon's strategic interests. And it was these expedient convictions that, to varying degrees, helped steer Amazon through the period of its greatest public scrutiny yet.

While the recession was in many ways a gift to Amazon, the deteriorating finances of local governments in the United States and Europe prompted a new fight over the collection of sales tax — the legal avoidance of which was one of the company's biggest tactical advantages. It was a high-stakes battle where there were more than two sides, no one played it entirely straight, and Amazon's deeply held convictions just happened to be conveniently expedient for its own long-term interests.

Beginning in late 2007, when governor of New York Eliot Spitzer introduced a proposal to raise millions of dollars by expanding the definition of what constituted a taxable presence in his state, Amazon was faced with the disconcerting possibility that its long exemption from adding 5 to 10 percent in sales tax onto the prices of most of its products — which had shaped its earliest decisions about where to conduct operations and place its headquarters — was about to end.

Spitzer's proposal flopped, at first. He withdrew it the day after introducing it, amid his own slumping approval ratings and a backlash over what his budget director said was concern that residents might consider the bill a tax increase.[3] But New York State had a

$4.3 billion budget gap that desperately needed to be filled. The following February, a month before Spitzer's political career imploded in a prostitution scandal, Spitzer reintroduced the bill. David Paterson, his successor, embraced the proposal, and in April it was passed by the state legislature in Albany.

The law cleverly eluded a 1992 Supreme Court ruling, *Quill v. North Carolina,* stipulating that only those merchants who had a physical presence or nexus, like a storefront or an office, in a state had to collect sales tax there. (Technically, the tax was still due for online purchases, but customers were supposed to pay it themselves.) The New York law specified that an affiliate website that took a commission for passing customers on to an online retailer was an agent of that retailer, and thus the retailer officially had a presence in that affiliate's state. By this ruling, if a Yankees-fan website in New York made money every time a visitor clicked a link on its pages and bought former manager Joe Torre's memoir on Amazon .com, then Seattle-based Amazon had an official storefront in New York and so had to collect sales tax on all purchases made in that state.

Amazon was not amused. The New York law went into effect over the summer of 2008 and, along with Overstock.com, another retailer, it sued in state court—and lost. Publicly, the company complained that state-by-state tax collection was complex and impractical. "There are currently about seventy-six hundred different jurisdictions in the country that tax, including things like snow-removal and mosquito-abatement districts," says Paul Misener, Amazon's vice president of global public policy and the public face of its tax battles.

Amazon had avoided sales-tax collection for years with various clever tricks. In states where it had fulfillment centers or other offices, like Lab126, it skirted the definition of what constituted a physical presence by classifying those facilities as wholly owned subsidiaries that earned no revenue. For example, the fulfillment center in Fernley, Nevada, operated as an independent entity called Amazon.com.nvdc, Inc. These arrangements were unlikely to hold up under direct scrutiny, but Amazon had carefully negotiated with each state when opening its facilities, securing hands-off treatment in exchange for the company's generating new jobs and economic activity. Bezos considered his exemption from collecting sales tax to be an enormous strategic advantage and brought a libertarian's earnestness to what he believed was a battle over principle. "We're not actually benefiting from any services that those states provide locally, so it's not fair that we should be obligated to be their tax collection agent since we're not getting any of the services," he said at a shareholder meeting in 2008.

Bezos also thought his exemption from collecting sales tax was a big benefit for customers, and the prospect of losing it triggered his apoplectic reaction to raising prices. He had good reason to be worried about the effects of sales-tax collection. When New York passed its Internet sales-tax law, Amazon's sales in New York State dropped 10 percent over the next quarter, according to a person familiar with Amazon's finances at the time.

New York's law spread like a bad cold. Similarly cash-strapped states like Illinois, North Carolina, Hawaii, Rhode Island, and Texas tried the same bank-shot approach of declaring that affiliate websites constituted nexuses. In response, Amazon borrowed a hardnosed tactic that Overstock had used in New York and severed ties with its affiliates in each state. These sites were often run by bloggers and other entrepreneurs who needed their affiliate commissions, and they were angered to find themselves wedged between a cash-starved state government on one side and an online giant belligerently clinging to a blatant tax loophole on the other.

The affiliates were not the only victims at this stage of the sales-tax fight. Vadim Tsypin was an Amazon engineer who often worked from his home in Quebec, Canada. In late 2007, around the time Eliot Spitzer was proposing his tax bill and Amazon's lawyers were growing more anxious, Tsypin's manager showed him the company's restrictive Canada policy, which declared that Amazon had no employees working in that country. His manager allegedly told Tsypin they had to cover up his history of working from home and, according to court documents, said that "Amazon can have multimillion-dollar problems. If we have even one employee on the ground there, it is a big violation of U.S. and Canadian law."

Tsypin refused to alter his old time sheets and evaluations, believing that it wouldn't stand up to scrutiny. He claimed that his Amazon bosses then started to harass him into quitting, which led to his getting sick ("constant migraine headaches and frequent seizure-like blackouts") and taking a medical leave of absence. In 2010, he sued Amazon in King County Superior Court for wrongful termination, breach of contract, emotional distress, and negligent hiring—and he lost. The judge acknowledged Tsypin's condition was work related but said the claims were not strong enough to impose a civil liability.

Large companies like Amazon are frequent targets of wrongful-termination claims. But Vadim Tsypin's case was unusual because it grew out of Amazon's own growing sales-tax anxieties and because the discovery phase brought Amazon's extensive tax-avoidance playbook into the public record. Dozens of pages of internal company rulebooks, flowcharts, and maps were filed with the King County Superior Court on Third Avenue in downtown Seattle. Together, they revealed a fascinating portrait of a company desperately contorting itself to accommodate a rapidly shifting tax climate.

The guidelines approached the surreal. Amazon employees had to seek approval to attend trade shows and were told to avoid activities that involved promoting the sale of any products on the Amazon website while on the road. They couldn't blog or talk to the press without permission, had to avoid renting any property on trips, and couldn't place orders on Amazon from the company's computers. They could sign contracts with other companies, such as suppliers who were offering their goods for sale on the site, only in Seattle.

Then the seemingly arbitrary partitions in the company's corporate structure became even more important. Traveling employees working for Amazon's North American retail organization were told to say they worked for a company called Amazon Services, not Amazon.com, and to carry business cards to that effect. According to one document, they were instructed to say, "I'm with Amazon Services, the operator of the www.amazon.com website and provider of e-commerce solutions and services, and I'm here to gather information about the latest industry developments and trends," if they were ever queried by the media regarding their attendance at a trade show.

Color-coded maps were widely distributed to employees at headquarters in Seattle. Travel to green states like Michigan was okay, but orange states like California required special clearance so that the legal department could track the cumulative number of days Amazon employees spent there. Travel to red states, like Texas, New Jersey, and Massachusetts, required employees to complete an intensive seventeen-item questionnaire about the trip that was designed to determine whether they would make the company vulnerable to sales-tax collection efforts (number 16: "Will you be holding a raffle?"). Amazon lawyers then either nixed the trip altogether or obtained a private letter ruling from that state spelling out its specific treatment of that particular situation.

There was little internal discussion by management on whether it was right or wrong or if it was affecting morale among employees, according to senior employees at the time. It was just strategy, a way to preserve a significant tax advantage that enabled the company to offer comparatively low prices. "The economic outlook for many states is bleak," read one early 2010 internal tax memo to employees that was filed in the Vadim Tsypin case record. "As a result, states are pursuing taxpayers more aggressively than before. Amazon's recent public experiences with New York and Texas provide timely and pertinent examples of the heightened risk. That's why our attention to nexus-related issues are more important than ever."[4]

That same year, 2010, fully alerted to the urgency of combating the Amazon threat, Walmart, Target, Best Buy, Home Depot, and Sears put aside their traditional enmities to join forces in an unusual coalition.⁵ They jointly backed a new organization called the Alliance for Main Street Fairness, which shrouded itself in populist language and—somehow managing to conceal the dripping irony—touted the importance of preserving the vitality of small mom-and-pop retailers. The organization employed a team of well-financed lobbyists who set up a sophisticated website and ran print and television ads around the country. The CEOs of all these big retailers monitored the campaign closely. Mike Duke, Walmart's CEO, requested frequent briefings on the sales-tax fight, according to two lobbyists involved in the battle.

Amazon fought the sales-tax expansion aggressively, soliciting cooperation from politicians by deploying both carrot and stick in the area where they might feel it most—jobs. In Texas in 2011, the legislature passed a bill that would force online retailers with distribution facilities in the state to collect sales tax, and Amazon threatened to close its fulfillment center outside Dallas, fire hundreds of local workers, and scrap plans to build other facilities in the state. Texas governor Rick Perry promptly vetoed the bill. In South Carolina, Amazon won an exemption on a new law by using the same threats, and it agreed to send customers e-mails helpfully reminding them they were supposed to pay sales tax on their own. In Tennessee, legislators agreed to delay a bill when Amazon offered to build three new fulfillment centers in the state.

During these skirmishes, Bezos advocated for a federal bill that simplified the sales tax code and imposed it over the entire e-commerce industry. (This had the advantage of being a highly unlikely scenario, considering the political deadlock gripping Washington, DC, at the time.) "If I say to customers, 'We're not required to collect sales tax, the Constitution is crystal clear that states cannot force out-of-state retailers to collect sales tax and cannot interfere in interstate commerce, but we're going to do it voluntarily anyway,' that isn't tenable," Bezos told me in a 2011 interview. "Customers would rightly protest. The way this has to work is you either have to amend the Constitution or you have to pass federal legislation."

The fight came to a dramatic head in 2012. Amazon surrendered in Texas, South Carolina, Pennsylvania, and Tennessee, negotiating accommodations that allowed it to stay tax-free for a few more years in exchange for putting new fulfillment centers in each state. In California, the most populous state, where the company apparently thought it could stave off the inevitable, Amazon girded itself for a fight. After the state legislature passed its sales-tax bill, Amazon engineered a campaign to overturn the law with a ballot measure and spent $5.25 million gathering signatures and running radio advertisements. Observers projected the company would have to spend over $50 million to see the fight through to the end.[6]

It quickly became evident that such a battle would be expensive, bitterly contested — and vicious. The Alliance for Main Street Fairness carpet-bombed the state with anti-Amazon advertisements, and editorial writers and bloggers largely sided with the big-box chains. "Amazon's attempt to avoid sales tax is one more sad example of the short-term thinking that rules American business," blogged Web evangelist Tim O'Reilly, knowing just how to push the buttons of Bezos, who prided himself on long-term thinking.[7] Inside Amazon, it was increasingly clear that the company was being fitted for the black hat of the bad guy. At the same time, Amazon was preparing to confront Apple in the high-stakes tablet market with the Kindle Fire. Colleagues insisted to Bezos that Amazon could not afford to see its brand tarnished at such a critical juncture.

So that fall, Amazon reversed course and reached an agreement with California: the company would drop its ballot measure in exchange for one more tax-free Christmas season, and it promised to build new fulfillment centers outside San Francisco and Los Angeles.[8] Soon after, Paul Misener testified before the Senate Commerce Science and Transportation Committee and reiterated Amazon's support for a federal bill — as did Amazon's unlikely new bedfellows in the sales-tax battle, Best Buy, Target, and Walmart. Now eBay, another combatant in the sales-tax wars, stood alone in trying to protect its smallest merchants, like the stay-at-home mother bringing in extra money by selling handmade mosaics. It advocated that the law should not apply to businesses with fewer than fifty employees or less than $10 million in annual sales, though most of the proposed national sales-tax bills put the exemption at less than $1 million. As of this writing, a national sales-tax-collection bill has not yet passed both houses of Congress.

Amazon was losing a sizable advantage, but Bezos, ever the farsighted chess player, was compensating by cultivating new ones. Amazon's new fulfillment centers would be close to large cities, allowing for the possibility of next-day or same-day delivery and the wider rollout of its grocery business, Amazon Fresh. Amazon also expanded its test of Amazon Lockers — large, orange locked cabinets placed in supermarkets, drugstores, and chains like Radio Shack that customers could have their Amazon packages shipped to if they liked.

As the era of tax-free online purchases was ending in many states, the true architect of Amazon's tax strategy and chief of its eighty-person tax department, an attorney named Robert Comfort, stepped out of the shadows. Comfort, a Princeton alumnus who joined Amazon in 2000, had spent more than a decade employing every trick in the book, and inventing many new ones, to minimize the company's tax burden. He created its controversial tax structure in Europe, funneling sales through entities in Luxembourg, which has a famously low tax rate. In 2012, this arcane tax structure nearly collapsed amid a wave of populist European anger directed at Amazon and other U.S. companies, including Google, who were trying to minimize their overseas tax burden.

Comfort announced his retirement and left Amazon in early 2012, just as the taxman was catching up with the company. (He has since taken a new job — a titular position as Seattle's honorary consul for the Grand Duchy of Luxembourg.)

And for the first time in its history, Amazon would have to fight its offline rivals on a level playing field.

*　　*　　*

There is a clandestine group inside Amazon with a name seemingly drawn from a James Bond film: Competitive Intelligence. The group, which since 2007 has operated within the finance department under longtime executives Tim Stone and Jason Warnick, buys large volumes of products from competitors and measures the quality and speed of their services. Its mandate is to investigate whether any rival is doing a better job than Amazon and then present the data to a committee that usually includes Bezos, Jeff Wilke, and Diego Piacentini, who ensure that the company addresses any emerging threat and catches up quickly.

In the late 2000s, Competitive Intelligence began tracking a rival with a difficult to pronounce name and a strong rapport with female shoppers. Quidsi (*quid si* is Latin for "what if") was a New Jersey company known for its website Diapers.com. Grammar-school friends Marc Lore and Vinit Bharara founded the startup in 2005 to allow sleep-deprived caregivers to painlessly schedule recurring shipments of vital supplies. By 2008, the company had expanded into selling all of the necessary survival gear for new parents, including baby wipes, infant formula, clothes, and strollers.

Dragging screaming children to the store is a well-known parental hassle, but Amazon didn't start selling diapers until a year after Diapers.com, and neither Walmart.com nor Target.com was investing significantly in the category. Back when the dark clouds of the dot-com bust still hung over the e-commerce industry, retailers felt that they wouldn't make any money shipping big, bulky, low-margin products like jumbo packs of Huggies Snug and Dry to people's front doors.

Lore and Bharara made it work by customizing their distribution system for baby gear. Quidsi's fulfillment centers, designed by former Boeing operations manager Scott Hilton, used software to match every order with the smallest possible shipping box (there were twenty-three sizes available), minimizing excess weight and thus reducing the per-order shipping cost. (Amazon, which had to match box sizes to a much larger selection of products, was not as adept at this.) Quidsi selected warehouses outside major population centers to take advantage of inexpensive ground-shipping rates and was able to promise free overnight shipping in two-thirds of the country. The Quidsi founders studied Amazon closely and idolized Jeff Bezos, referring to him in private conversation as "sensei."[9]

Moms got hooked on the seemingly magical appearance of diapers on their doorsteps and enthusiastically told friends about Diapers.com. Several venture-capital firms, including Accel Partners, a backer of Facebook, bought into the possibility that Lore and Bharara had identified a weakness in Amazon's armor, and they pumped over $50 million into the company. Around this time, Jeff Bezos and his business-development team, as well as Amazon's counterparts at Walmart, started to pay attention.

Executives and official representatives from Amazon, Quidsi, and Walmart have all declined to discuss the ensuing scuffle in detail. Jeff Blackburn, Amazon's mergers and acquisitions chief, said Quidsi was similar to Zappos, a "stubbornly independent company building an extremely flexible franchise." He also said that everything Amazon subsequently did in the diapers market was planned beforehand and was unrelated to competing with Quidsi.

The story that follows has been pieced together from the recollections of insiders at all three companies. They spoke anonymously and with a significant amount of trepidation, given the strength of Amazon's and Walmart's strict nondisclosure agreements and the possibility of legal consequences for them for speaking publically about it.

In 2009, Blackburn ominously informed the Quidsi cofounders over an introductory lunch that the e-commerce giant was getting ready to invest in the category and that the startup should think seriously about selling to Amazon. Lore and Bharara replied that they wanted to remain private and build an independent company. Blackburn told the Quidsi founders that they should call him if they ever reconsidered.

Soon after, Quidsi noticed Amazon dropping prices up to 30 percent on diapers and other baby products. As an experiment, Quidsi execs manipulated their prices and then watched as Amazon's website changed its prices accordingly. Amazon's famous pricing bots were lasered in on Diapers.com.

Quidsi fared well under Amazon's assault, at least at first. It didn't try to match Amazon's low prices but capitalized on the strength of its brand and continued to reap the benefits of strong word of mouth. It also used its trusting relationship with customers and its expertise in fulfillment to open two new websites, Soap.com for home goods and BeautyBar.com for makeup. But after a while, the heated competition began to take a toll on the company. Quidsi had grown from nothing to $300 million in annual sales in just a few years, but with Amazon focusing on the category, revenue growth started to slow. Investors were reluctant to furnish Quidsi with additional capital, and the company was not yet mature enough for an IPO. For the first time, Lore and Bharara had to think about selling.

At around this point, Walmart was looking for ways to make up the ground they'd lost to Amazon, and the retailer was shaking up its online division. Walmart vice chairman Eduardo Castro-Wright took over Walmart.com, and one of his first calls was to Marc Lore at Diapers.com to initiate acquisition talks. Lore said that Quidsi wanted a chance to get "Zappos money"—$900 million, which included bonuses spread out over many years tied to performance goals. Walmart agreed in principle and started due diligence. Mike Duke, Walmart's CEO, even visited a Diapers.com fulfillment center in New Jersey. However, the subsequent formal offer from Bentonville was well under the requested amount.

So Lore picked up the phone and called Amazon. On September 14, 2010, Lore and Bharara traveled to Seattle to pitch Jeff Bezos on acquiring Quidsi. While they were in that early-morning meeting with Bezos, Amazon sent out a press release introducing a new service called Amazon Mom. It was a sweet deal for new parents: they could get up to a year's worth of free two-day Prime shipping (a program that usually cost $79 to join), and there was a wealth of other perks available, including an additional 30 percent off the already-discounted diapers, if they signed up for regular monthly deliveries of diapers as part of a service called Subscribe and Save. Back in New Jersey, Quidsi employees desperately tried to call their founders to discuss a public response to Amazon Mom. It was no accident that they couldn't reach them. They were sitting blithely unaware in a meeting in Amazon's own offices.

Quidsi could now taste its own blood. That month, Diapers.com listed a case of Pampers at forty-five dollars; Amazon priced it at thirty-nine dollars, and Amazon Mom customers with Subscribe and Save could get a case for less than thirty dollars.[10] At one point, Quidsi executives took what they knew about shipping rates, factored in Procter and Gamble's wholesale prices, and calculated that Amazon was on track to lose $100 million over three months in the diapers category alone.

Inside Amazon, Bezos had rationalized these moves as being in the company's long-term interest of delighting its customers and building its consumables business. He told business-development vice president Peter Krawiec not to spend over a certain amount to buy Quidsi but to make sure that Amazon did not, under any circumstances, lose the deal to Walmart.

As a result of Bezos's meeting with Lore and Bharara, Amazon now had an exclusive three-week period to study Quidsi's financial results and come up with a proposal. At the end of that period, Krawiec offered Quidsi $540 million and said that this was a "stretch price." Knowing that Walmart hovered on the sidelines, he gave Quidsi a window of forty-eight hours to respond and made it clear that if the founders didn't take the offer, the heightened competition would continue.

Walmart should have had a natural advantage in this fight. Jim Breyer, the managing partner at one of Quidsi's venture-capital backers, Accel, was also on the Walmart board of directors. But Walmart was caught flat-footed. By the time Walmart upped its offer to $600 million, Quidsi had tentatively accepted the Amazon term sheet. Mike Duke called and left messages for several Quidsi board members, imploring them not to sell to Amazon. Those messages were then transcribed and sent to Seattle, since Amazon had stipulated in the preliminary term sheet that Quidsi was required to turn over information about any subsequent offers.

When Amazon executives learned of Walmart's counterbid, they ratcheted up the pressure even further, threatening the Quidsi founders that "sensei," being such a furious competitor, would drive diaper prices to zero if they went with Walmart. The Quidsi board convened to discuss the Amazon proposal and the possibility of letting it expire and then resuming negotiations with Walmart. But by then, Bezos's Khrushchev-like willingness to take the e-commerce equivalent of the thermonuclear option in the diaper price war made Quidsi worried that it would be exposed and vulnerable if something went wrong during the consummation of a shotgun marriage to Walmart. So the Quidsi executives stuck with Amazon, largely out of fear. The deal was announced on November 8, 2010.

The money-losing Amazon Mom program was obviously introduced to help dead-end Diapers.com and force a sale, and if anyone at the time had doubts about that, those doubts were quickly dispelled by Amazon's subsequent actions.

A month after it announced the acquisition of Quidsi, Amazon closed the program to new members. But by then the Federal Trade Commission was reviewing the deal, and a few weeks after it closed the program, Amazon reversed course and reopened it, though with much smaller discounts.

The Federal Trade Commission scrutinized the acquisition for four and a half months, going beyond the standard review to the second-request phase, where companies must provide more information about a transaction. The deal raised a host of red flags, according to an FTC official familiar with the review. A significant head-to-head competition and the subsequent merger had led to the demise of a major player in the category. But the deal was eventually approved, in part because it did not result in a monopoly. There was a plethora of other companies, like Costco and Target, that sold diapers both online and offline.

Bezos had won again, neutralizing an incipient competitor and filling another set of shelves in his everything store. Like Zappos, Quidsi was permitted to operate independently within Amazon (from New Jersey), and soon it expanded into pet supplies with Wag.com and toys with Yoyo.com. Walmart had missed the chance to acquire a talented team of entrepreneurs who had gone toe to toe with Amazon in a key product category. And insiders were once again left with their mouths agape, marveling at how Bezos had ruthlessly engineered another acquisition by driving his target off a cliff. Says one observer who had a seat close to the battle, "They have an absolute willingness to torch the landscape around them to emerge the winner."

*   *   *

Anxiety over Amazon isn't restricted to New Jersey, Las Vegas, and other American places. The industrial city of Solingen, Germany, halfway between Düsseldorf and Cologne, is famous for the production of high-quality razors and knives. The local blacksmith trade dates back two millennia, and today the city is the seat of the European knife industry and home to renowned brands like Wüsthof, a two-hundred-year-old firm that's been run by seven successive generations of the Wüsthof family. In the 1960s, Wolfgang Wüsthof introduced the company's high-end products to North America, riding a bus from town to town with a suitcase full of knives. Forty years later, his grandnephew Harald Wüsthof took over the firm and started selling to chains like Williams-Sonoma and Macy's. Then, in the early 2000s, Wüsthof began supplying its wares to Amazon.com.

Over the course of its fifty years in America, Wüsthof has established itself as a premium brand, winning frequent commendations from the likes of *Consumer Reports* and *Cook's Illustrated*. For that reason it can charge a hundred and twenty-five dollars for an eight-inch hollow-ground cook's knife made of high-carbon laser-tested steel, even though similar-size kitchen knives sell for twenty dollars each at Target. Maintaining that lofty price is vital for a company that employs hundreds of skilled artisans in its factory but that competes in a category full of inferior products that, to an untrained eye, all look roughly the same.

Which is why Amazon's five-year association with Wüsthof—like its relationship with so many brands and manufacturers around the world—has been about as bloody as an actual knife fight.

Manufacturers are not allowed to enforce retail prices for their products. But they can decide which retailers to sell to, and one way they wield that power is by setting price floors with a tool called MAP, or minimum advertised price. MAP requires offline retailers like Walmart to stay above a certain price threshold in their circulars and newspaper ads. Online retailers have a higher burden. Their product pages are considered advertisements, so they have to set their promoted prices at or above MAP or else face the manufacturer's wrath and risk the firm's limiting the number of products allocated or withdrawing them altogether.

Over its first few years selling Wüsthof knives, Amazon respected the German firm's pricing wishes. Amazon was a good partner, placing large orders as its traffic grew and settling its bills on time. It quickly became Wüsthof's top online retailer and second-largest U.S. seller overall, after Williams-Sonoma. Then tensions in the relationship emerged. As Amazon pricing-bot software got better at scouring the Web and finding and matching low prices elsewhere, Amazon repeatedly violated Wüsthof's MAP requirements, selling products like the $125 Grand Prix chef's knife for $109. Wüsthof felt it needed MAP to defend the value of its brand and protect the small independent knife shops that were responsible for about a quarter of the company's sales and were not capable of matching such discounts. "These are the guys that built my brand," says René Arnold, the CFO of Wüsthof-Trident of America. "Amazon cannot sell a new knife. They can't explain it like a store."

Wüsthof finally stopped allocating products to Amazon in 2006. "It was painful for us," Arnold says. "Those were lost sales, at least in the short term. But we believed our product and our brand were stronger than the brand of our distributors." For the next three years—until 2009, when Wüsthof changed its mind and initiated part two of its tortured relationship with Amazon—Wüsthof knives were absent from the shelves of the everything store.

Companies that make things and companies that sell them have waged versions of this battle for centuries. With its commitment to everyday low prices and the ingenious marriage of direct retail with a third-party marketplace, Amazon has taken these historic tensions to a new level. Like Sam Walton, Bezos sees it as his company's mission to drive inefficiencies out of the supply chain and deliver the lowest possible price to its customers. Amazon executives view MAPs and similar techniques as the last vestiges of an old way of doing business, gimmicks that inefficient companies use to protect their bloated margins. Amazon has come up with countless workarounds, including a technique called hide the price. In some cases, when Amazon breaks MAP, it doesn't list the price on its product page. A customer can see the low price only when he places the item in his shopping cart.

It's an inelegant solution, driven by Amazon's age-old desire to have the lowest prices anywhere and the novel ability of its pricing algorithms to quickly match any major seller that goes lower. "We know it's in the customer's best interest that we have a cost structure that allows us to match competitors and be known for low prices," says Jeff Wilke. "That's our objective." Wilke acknowledges that not everyone is happy with this approach but says Amazon is consistent about it and that manufacturers should understand that it is the nature of the Internet itself—not just Amazon—that allows customers to easily find the lowest price.

"If vendors or brands leave Amazon, they will eventually come back," Wilke predicts, because "customers trust Amazon to be great providers of information and customer reviews about a vast selection of products. If you have customers ready to buy, and if you have a chance to tell them about your product, what brand ultimately doesn't want that?"

Dyson, the British vacuum maker, is one example of a brand that appears to treat Amazon with caution. It sold on Amazon for years and then an irate Sir James Dyson, its founder, visited Amazon's offices personally to vent his frustrations over repeated violations of

MAP. "Sir James said he trusted us with his brand and we had violated that trust," says Kerry Morris, a former senior buyer who hosted Dyson on that memorable visit. Dyson pulled its vacuums from Amazon in 2011, though some models are still sold on the Amazon Marketplace by approved third-party merchants. Over the past few years, companies such as Sony and Black and Decker have taken turns yanking various products from the site. Apple in particular keeps Amazon on a tight leash, giving it a limited supply of iPods but no iPads or iPhones.

Amazon's booming marketplace is a primary source of tension between Amazon and other companies. Over the holiday months in 2012, 39 percent of products sold on Amazon were brokered over its third-party marketplace, up from 36 percent the year before. The company said that over two million third-party sellers worldwide used Amazon Marketplace and that they sold 40 percent more products in 2012 than in 2011.[11] The Marketplace business is a profitable one for the company, since it takes a flat 6 to 15 percent commission on each sale and does not bear the expense of buying and holding the inventory.

Some of the retailers who sell via the Amazon Marketplace seem to have a schizophrenic relationship with the company, particularly if they have no unique and sustainable selling point, such as an exclusive on a particular product. Amazon closely monitors what they sell, notices any briskly selling items, and often starts selling those products itself. By paying Amazon commissions and helping it source hot products, retailers on the Amazon Marketplace are in effect aiding their most ferocious competitor.

In 2003, Michael Ross was chief executive of Figleaves.com, a London-based online lingerie and swimwear site that sold popular sports bras made by the British brand Shock Absorber. Figleaves had Amazon's attention early on. To promote the company's debut in the United States on Amazon's Marketplace, Ross helped arrange a lopsided exhibition tennis match between Jeff Bezos and Shock Absorber's celebrity endorser Anna Kournikova.

Figleaves sold its wares on Amazon's Marketplace for a few years but left unhappily at the end of 2008. By then, Amazon.com was carrying a wide assortment of Shock Absorber bras and swimsuits, and Figleaves was selling very little on the site. "In a world where consumers had limited choice, you needed to compete for locations," says Ross, who went on to cofound eCommera, a British e-commerce advisory firm. "But in a world where consumers have unlimited choice, you need to compete for attention. And this requires something more than selling other people's products."

Even sellers who thrive in Amazon's Marketplace tend to regard it warily. GreenCupboards, a seller of environmentally responsible products, like eco-friendly laundry detergents and pet supplies, has built a sixty-person company almost entirely via Amazon, despite the fact that founder Josh Neblett says that Marketplace enables "a race to zero." His company is constantly competing with other sellers and with Amazon's own retail organization to provide the lowest possible price and to capture the "buy box" — to be the default seller of a particular product on the site. That furious price competition tends to drive prices down and eliminate profit margin. As a result, GreenCupboards has had to get more Amazon-like to survive. Neblett says the company has gotten better at sourcing hot new products, locking up exclusives, and building a lean organization. "I've just always considered it a game and we are figuring out how to best play it," he says.

Still, as Wilke says, some of the companies that disavow selling on Amazon ultimately return, irresistibly drawn to its 200 million active customers and brisk sales. Amazon's own employees have compared third-party selling on the site to heroin addiction — sellers get a sudden euphoric rush and a lingering high as sales explode, then progress to addiction and self-destruction when Amazon starts gutting the sellers' margins and undercutting them on price. Sellers "know they should not be taking the heroin, but they cannot stop taking the heroin," says Kerry Morris, the former Amazon buyer. "They push and bitch and complain and threaten until they finally see they have to cut themselves off."

Wüsthof, the German knife maker, had its relapse in 2009, after an intensive courtship by Amazon that included promises of obedience in regard to the manufacturer's suggested price. The company reallocated product to the online retailer, but the earlier pattern repeated itself; for example, Wüsthof's gourmet twelve-piece knife set, with a MAP of $199, showed up on the site at $179. René Arnold, the CFO, was overwhelmed with complaints from his other retail partners, whose prices remained 10 percent higher. These small shop owners either lost sales to Amazon or were forced by their customers to match Amazon's price. In their angry calls to Arnold, they threatened to lower their retail prices as well, and now it was easy for Arnold and his colleagues to envision a day when all these retailers would start demanding lower wholesale prices on Wüsthof knives, cutting into the company's profit margins. The economics of its traditional-manufacturing operation in Germany would no longer make sense.

When Arnold complained, his counterpart at Amazon, a merchandising manager named Kevin Bates, responded that the company was merely finding and matching lower prices on the Web and in its third-party Marketplace. Arnold argued that many of those sellers were not authorized retailers and urged Amazon not to match them. Bates said that he was required to — Amazon always matched the lowest price.

Arnold was frustrated. He was monitoring Amazon's third-party Marketplace and tracking several unfamiliar low-priced sellers, including one called Great Deals Now Online. This mysterious entity always seemed to have Wüsthof knives for sale, yet Arnold had no idea who they were, and Amazon provided no way to contact them. "He might know someone who has gotten a hold of surplus product, or he might have someone working at Bed, Bath and Beyond stealing from the distribution center," says Arnold. "Customers would never give their credit card to this guy, but because he's on the Amazon platform, they figure he's clean, he must be good." Arnold felt that Amazon's own Marketplace was enabling the destructive discounting that its retail business was using as an excuse to undercut MAP.

In 2011, Wüsthof decided, again, to end its relationship with Amazon. To help explain to his bosses why Wüsthof was cutting off one of its best sales channels, René Arnold requested a meeting with Amazon and brought Harald Wüsthof over from Germany. Wüsthof, in his mid-forties with wavy, white hair and an avuncular smile, has quite possibly never in his life been photographed without a sharp blade in his hands.

The meeting, at Amazon's offices in Seattle, was tense. Kevin Bates was joined by his boss Dan Joy, a director of hard-line categories like kitchen and dining. Bates and Joy seemed genuinely surprised to hear that Wüsthof was walking away and vowed to acquire Wüsthof knives through the gray market. They also threatened the company, as Arnold recalls, saying that every time a customer searched on Amazon for the Wüsthof brand, Amazon would show advertisements for competitors like J. A. Henckels, another knife company based in Solingen, and Victorinox, maker of Swiss army knives.

Wüsthof and Arnold were shocked by the fierceness of Amazon's stance and held firm on their decision to withdraw. "Anyone can sell more Wüsthof at half the price. It's easy," Arnold says. "But if you start selling at the lower price, maybe you have a heyday for a few years, but within two or three years you drive a two-hundred-year-old family business into a wall. We had to protect our brand. That was the main decision point. So we pulled out."

At a kitchen-and-bath trade show in Chicago the following spring, Arnold was surprised to receive an outpouring of support from sympathetic vendors who were also tussling with Amazon over issues like MAPs and mysterious third-party sellers. Meanwhile, Amazon followed through on its threats to show ads for Wüsthof rivals. In mid-2012, an enterprising Amazon buyer somehow managed to get someone at Wüsthof headquarters in Germany to ship him a large crate of knives meant to go to Dubai. That supply lasted about six weeks.

By the end of 2012, an Amazon merchandising representative began courting Wüsthof once more, begging the company to reconsider. The knife maker declined. But here's the kicker: Customers can still find a decent selection of Wüsthof knives on Amazon from a handful of third-party sellers and even from Amazon itself. In 2010, Amazon started a unit called Warehouse Deals. The unit buys refurbished and used products and sells them in the Amazon Marketplace and on the Web at Warehousedeals.com. The goal of the project, according to an executive who worked on it, is to become the largest liquidator on the planet. These products are often advertised as "good as new"—a package of diapers with a tear in the shrink wrap, for example—and Amazon is not required to sell them at MAP.

As of this writing, Warehouse Deals has a selection of more than sixty Wüsthof products at steep discounts. Third-party merchants, mostly other authorized Wüsthof retailers, also sell their knives on Amazon, often through Fulfillment by Amazon, which allows the products to qualify for Prime shipping. So even when partners flee, the groundwork that Amazon has laid ensures that the hallowed shelves of the everything store are never completely bare.

*   *   *

Back in the anxious years after the dot-com bust, when Wüsthof was still happily selling its knives on Amazon.com, Jeff Bezos was tracking a firm he viewed as a potentially dangerous new rival: Netflix. At the time, Amazon was making a little extra money by inserting paper advertisements into its delivery boxes, and Bezos himself received a package that contained a flyer for the DVD-rental firm. He brought the flyer into a meeting and said irritably of the managers running the advertising program, "Is it easy for them to ruin the company or do they have to work at it?"

Bezos was clearly nervous about Netflix's gathering momentum. With its recognizable red envelopes and late-fee-slaying DVD-by-mail program, it was forging a bond with customers and a strong brand in movies, a key media category. Bezos's lieutenants met with CEO Reed Hastings several times during Netflix's formative years but they always reported back that Hastings was "painfully uninterested" in selling, according to one Amazon business-development exec. Hastings himself says that Amazon was never truly serious about an acquisition of Netflix because "the basic operating rhythms" of the DVD-rental space, which required multiple small fulfillment centers to send discs out and then receive them back, were so different from Amazon's core retail business. "It made no sense for them to be an aggressive bidder because it didn't really leverage their strengths," he says.

Like everyone else, Amazon executives knew that the days of selling and shipping physical DVDs were numbered, but they wanted to be prepared and well positioned for whatever came next. So Amazon opened DVD-rental services in the United Kingdom and Germany, with the idea that it would learn the rental business and establish its brand in markets that Netflix had not yet entered. But local companies were ahead there too, and the cost to acquire new customers was higher than Amazon had anticipated. In February 2008, Amazon seemingly waved the white flag of surrender, selling those divisions to a larger competitor, Lovefilm, in exchange for about $90 million in stock and a 32 percent ownership position in the European firm. Jeff Blackburn says that by then Amazon suspected there was little future for the rental model and that "we sold them the DVD business because they seemed to be overvaluing it."

Lovefilm was a kind of Frankenstein corporate creation, the combination of numerous Netflix clones that had gradually merged with one other and come to control a majority of the British and German rental market. As a result, it had many shareholders (including several prominent venture-capital firms), a large board of directors, and plenty of conflicting internal opinions about its strategic moves. Amazon became the largest shareholder after the deal and later consolidated its grip on the startup when another investor, the European venture-capital firm Arts Alliance, sold the company a 10 percent stake. Greg Greeley, the former finance executive who was running Amazon's European operation, joined the Lovefilm board. As it is wont to do, Amazon watched from the sidelines, learned, and patiently waited for an opening.

By early 2009, the home-video market was inexorably tilting

toward streaming movies online and away from sending discs in the mail. Like Netflix, Lovefilm planned to transition to video on demand. It had arranged streaming deals with movie studios like Warner Brothers and put access to its catalog on devices like Sony's PlayStation 3. But the company needed additional capital to execute such a shift in its business, so that year it hired the investment bank Jefferies and started entertaining acquisition and investment offers.

While private equity firms like Silver Lake Partners expressed interest, Google was the most prominent bidder for Lovefilm. The search giant's executive team was developing a plan over the summer of 2009 to acquire both Lovefilm and Netflix and add a significant new focus that was unrelated to its core advertising business. Nikesh Arora and David Lawee, business-development executives at Google, had several meetings with people at both companies that year and produced a preliminary letter of Google's intent to buy Lovefilm for two hundred million pounds (about three hundred million dollars), according to three people with knowledge of the offer. But these efforts ultimately fizzled; there was opposition from Google's YouTube division and fear that the company might be able to acquire one streaming-video business but not the other.

That left Lovefilm still in need of additional capital. So over the summer of 2010, the company's executives decided to pursue an initial public offering. Then Amazon decided it wanted to buy Lovefilm, and everything changed.

Amazon had watched the explosion in popularity of Internet-connected Blu-ray players and video-game consoles in its own electronics store and knew it had to get off the sidelines. Its incipient streaming service, Amazon Video on Demand, was the successor to an overly complicated video download store called Amazon Unbox, which required users to download entire movies to their PCs or TiVo set-top boxes before they could start watching. The streaming service (which did not require downloads) was showing early promise but the company still lagged behind Apple and Hulu in the online-video market. Buying Lovefilm would give it a beachhead in Europe. "They went from having a financial interest, where they thought they might make a financial return on their investment, to a strategic interest," says Dharmash Mistry, a former partner at the London venture-capital firm Balderton Capital and a Lovefilm board member. "They wanted to own the asset."

Now the Lovefilm board members would witness the same ruthless tactics observed by the founders of Zappos and Quidsi. Amazon pointed out, quite sensibly, that Lovefilm needed to invest hundreds of millions to acquire content and hold off deep-pocketed rivals like the massive cable conglomerate BSkyB and, when it finally entered the European market, Netflix. Amazon also argued that Lovefilm needed to invest in its long-term prospects and should not spend time and money gussying itself up for the conservative public markets in Europe, which would want to see profits before an IPO. The best path forward was for Lovefilm to sell itself to Amazon. It was more Bezos-style expedient conviction — the arguments had the advantage of being completely rational while also serving Amazon's own strategic interests.

In the midst of this debate, Amazon found a technical way to prevent a Lovefilm IPO. If the company was going to free up stock to sell to the public, it needed to amend its own bylaws, or articles of association — and as the largest shareholder, Amazon could block this change. It effectively had a veto over an IPO, and Amazon made it clear that it was not going to authorize or publicly endorse the move, according to multiple board members and people close to the company. This was an enormous problem. Potential investors were likely to balk if the company's biggest shareholder was not visibly showing its support for the offering.

Lovefilm executives had several meetings with attorneys to try to find a way to extricate themselves from the situation. They also attempted to entice other potential acquirers, hoping to spark a bidding war, but without success. Everyone saw that Amazon was squatting over the asset.

Though Lovefilm was a prestigious European company with a strong brand and solid momentum, Amazon offered an opening bid of a hundred and fifty million pounds, the very bottom of Lovefilm price range. With no alternatives, Lovefilm started negotiating. In the protracted discussions that followed, Amazon characteristically argued every point, such as compensation packages for management and the timing of escrow payments. Lovefilm's attorneys were astonished at the intractable positions taken by Amazon's negotiators. The talks lasted more than seven months, and the acquisition was finally announced in January 2011. Amazon ended up paying close to two hundred million pounds, or about three hundred million dollars — roughly the same amount Google had offered despite the fact that Lovefilm had expanded its subscriber base and its digital catalog of movies in the intervening year and a half.

Amazon now had a strong foothold in the European video market just as it unveiled its most serious play for the living room. A month after it announced the purchase of Lovefilm, the company introduced a video-streaming service for Amazon Prime in the United States. Members of the two-day shipping service could watch for free a selection of movies and television shows, a catalog that would grow steadily over the next few years as Amazon inked deals with content providers such as CBS, NBC Universal, Viacom, and the pay-TV channel Epix.

Inside the company, Bezos rationalized the giveaway by saying that it sustained and even complemented the seventy-nine-dollar fee for Prime at a time when customers were buying fewer DVDs. But Prime Instant Video played another role. Amazon was now providing, as a supplementary perk, something Reed Hastings and his colleagues at Netflix priced at five to eight dollars a month. The service exerted direct pressure on a key rival and worked to prevent it from appropriating an important section of the everything store. Amazon too would offer films and TV shows in any form that customers could possibly want — all with the click of a button.

To Jeff Bezos, perhaps the only thing more sacrosanct than offering customers these kinds of choices was selling them products and services at the lowest possible prices. But in the fractious world of book publishing, Amazon, it seemed in early 2011, was losing its ability to set low prices. That March, Random House, the largest book publisher in the United States, followed the other big publishers and adopted the agency pricing model, which allowed them to set their own price for e-books and remit a 30 percent commission to retailers. Amazon executives had spent considerable time pleading in vain with their Random House counterparts to stick with the wholesale model. Bezos now no longer had control over a key part of the customer experience for some of the biggest books in the world.

With no stark price advantage and increased competition from Barnes & Noble's Nook, Apple's iBookstore, and the Toronto-based startup Kobo, Amazon's e-book market share fell from 90 percent in 2010 to around 60 percent in 2012. "For the first time, a level playing field was going to get forced on Amazon," says James Gray, the former chief strategy officer of the Ingram Content Group. Amazon executives "were basically spitting blood and nails."

Amazon felt major book publishers were limiting its ability to experiment with new digital formats. For example, the Kindle 2 was introduced with a novel text-to-speech function that read books aloud in a robotic male or female voice. Roy Blount Jr., the president of the Authors Guild, led a protest against the feature, writing an editorial for the *New York Times* that argued authors were not getting paid for audio rights.[12] Amazon backed off and allowed publishers and authors to enable the feature for specific titles; many declined.

Book publishers were refusing to play by Amazon's rules. So Amazon decided to reinvent the rulebook. It started a New York–based publishing imprint with the lofty ambition to publish best-selling books by big-name authors — the bread-and-butter of New York's two-century-old book industry.

In April of 2011, a month after Random House moved to the agency model, an Amazon recruiter sent e-mails to several accomplished editors at New York publishing houses. She was looking for someone to launch and oversee an imprint that "will focus on the acquisition of original commercially oriented fiction and non-fiction with the goal of becoming bestsellers," according to the e-mail. "This imprint will be supported with a large budget and its success will directly impact the success of Amazon's overall business." Most of the e-mail's recipients politely declined the offer, so Kindle vice president Jeff Belle asked the man who'd been steering him toward possible recruits if he himself might be interested in the job. "Well, the thought had crossed my mind," replied Larry Kirshbaum, a literary agent and, before that, the head of Time Warner's book division.

Kirshbaum, sixty-seven at the time, was the ultimate insider, widely known and, until then, almost universally liked. He had a well-honed instinct for big, mass-culture books and an intuitive feel for survival inside large corporations. When AOL acquired Time Warner in 2000, he directed the staff of Warner Books to wear I Heart AOL T-shirts and made a video of everyone standing around a piano singing "Unforgettable" (the company had just published Natalie Cole's autobiography). He was thinking about e-books — and losing money on them — long before almost anyone else in the industry.

Kirshbaum reentered a very different environment than the one he had left in 2005 when he departed AOL Time Warner to become an agent. Animosity toward Amazon had become a defining fact of life in the book business. So he was considered by many of his former peers to be a defector, someone who had gone over to the dark side, a sentiment they did not hesitate to express to him, sometimes in pointed terms.

"There have been a few brickbats I've had to duck," Kirshbaum says, "but I have a message I really believe in, which is that we're trying to innovate in ways that can help everybody. We are trying to create a tide that will lift all boats." He points to the industry's similarly negative reaction to Barnes & Noble's acquisition of the publisher

Sterling back in 2003, which raised the same fear that a powerful retailer was trying to monopolize the attention of readers. "We all worried the sun wasn't going to come up the next day, but it did," he says. Of Amazon, he says, "We certainly want to be a major player, but there are thousands of publishers and millions of books. I think it's a little bit of a stretch to say we are cornering the market."

Kirshbaum's bosses in Seattle sounded a similarly conciliatory note. "Our entire publishing business is an in-house laboratory that allows us to experiment toward the goal of finding new and interesting ways to connect authors and readers," Jeff Belle told me for a *Businessweek* cover story on Amazon Publishing in early 2012. "It's not our intention to become Random House or Simon & Schuster or HarperCollins. I think people have a hard time believing that."[13]

Amazon executives charged that the book publishers were irrationally consumed with the possibility of their own demise and noted that resisting changes, like paperback books and discount superstores, was something of a hallmark for the industry. And when it came to fielding questions on the topic, Amazon executives perfected a sort of passive-aggressive perplexity, insisting that the media was overplaying the issue and giving it undue attention — sometimes with explanations that compounded and confirmed publishers' concerns. "The iceman was a really important part of weekly American culture for years and his purpose was to keep your food from spoiling," says Donald Katz, the founder and chief executive of Amazon's Audible subsidiary. "But when refrigerators were invented, it was not about what the iceman thought, nor did anyone spend a lot of time writing about it."

Book publishers needed only to listen to Jeff Bezos himself to have their fears stoked. Amazon's founder repeatedly suggested he had little reverence for the old "gatekeepers" of the media, whose business models were forged during the analogue age and whose function it was to review content and then subjectively decide what the public got to consume. This was to be a new age of creative surplus, where it was easy for anyone to create something, find an audience, and allow the market to determine the proper economic reward. "Even well meaning gatekeepers slow innovation," Bezos wrote in his 2011 letter to shareholders. "When a platform is self-service, even the improbable ideas can get tried, because there's no expert gatekeeper ready to say 'that will never work!' And guess what—many of those improbable ideas do work, and society is the beneficiary of that diversity."

A few weeks after that letter was published, Bezos told Thomas Friedman of the *New York Times,* "I see the elimination of gatekeepers everywhere." In case there was any doubt about the nature of Bezos's convictions, Friedman then imagined a publishing world that includes "just an author, who gets most of the royalties, and Amazon and the reader."[14]

"At least it's all out in the open now," one well-known book agent said at the time.

A kind of industrywide immune response then kicked in. The book world rejected Amazon's new publishing efforts en masse. Barnes & Noble and most independent bookstores refused to stock Amazon's books, and New York–based media and publishing executives widely scoffed at the preliminary efforts of Kirshbaum and his fledgling editorial team. Their $800,000 acquisition of a memoir by actress and director Penny Marshall, for example, was targeted for particular ridicule and later sold poorly.

Meanwhile, Amazon continued to experiment with new e-book formats and push the boundaries of publishers' and authors' tolerance. It introduced the Kindle Single, a novella-length e-book format, and the Prime Lending Library, which allowed Prime members who owned a Kindle reading device to borrow one digital book a month for free. But Amazon included the books of many mid-tier publishers in its lending catalog without asking for permission, reasoning that it had purchased those books at wholesale and thus believed it could set any retail price it wished (including, in this case, zero). In the imbroglio that ensued, the Authors Guild called the lending library "an exercise of brute economic power," and Amazon backed off.[15]

Bezos and colleagues dismissed the early challenges Kirshbaum's

New York division faced and said they would gauge its success over the long term. They were likely positioning their direct-publishing efforts for a future where electronic books made up a majority of the publishing market and where chains like Barnes & Noble might not exist in their present form. In that world, Amazon alone will still be standing, publishing not just scrappy new writers but prominent brand-name authors as well. And Larry Kirshbaum could once again be one of the most popular—and possibly one of the only—publishing guys left in New York City.

*　　*　　*

In December of 2011, as if seeking a fitting conclusion to a year filled with controversy over sales tax, acquisitions, MAPs, and the economics of electronic books, Amazon ran a ham-fisted promotion of its price-comparison application for smartphones. The app allowed users to take pictures or scan the bar codes of products in local stores and compare those prices with Amazon's. On December 10, Amazon offered a discount of up to fifteen dollars to anyone who used the application to buy online instead of in a store. Although certain categories, like books, were exempt, the move stirred up an avalanche of criticism.

Senator Olympia Snowe called the promotion "anti-competitive" and "an attack on Main Street businesses that employ workers in our communities." An employee of Powell's Books in Portland, Oregon, created an Occupy Amazon page on Facebook. An Amazon spokesperson noted that the application was meant primarily for comparing the prices of big retail chains, but it didn't matter. The critics piled on, charging that Amazon was using its customers to spy on competitors' prices and was siphoning away the sales of mom-and-pop merchants. "I first attributed Amazon's price-comparison app to arrogance and malevolence, but there's also something bizarrely clumsy and wrong-footed about it," wrote the novelist Richard Russo in a scathing editorial for the *New York Times*.[16]

The conflagration over the price-checking app diminished quickly. But it raised larger questions: Would Amazon continue to be viewed as an innovative and value-creating company that existed to serve and delight its customers, or would it increasingly be seen as a monolith that merely transferred dollars out of the accounts of other companies and local communities and into its own gilded coffers?

During these years of conflict, Jeff Bezos sat down to consider this very question. When Amazon became a company with $100 billion in sales, he wondered, how could it be loved and not feared? As he regularly does, Bezos wrote up his thoughts in a memo and distributed it to his top executives at an S Team retreat. I received a copy through a person close to the company who wished to remain anonymous. The memo, which Bezos titled Amazon.love, lays out a vision for how the Amazon founder wants his company to conduct itself and be perceived by the world. It reflects Bezos's values and determination, and perhaps even his blind spots.

"Some big companies develop ardent fan bases, are widely loved by their customers, and are even perceived as cool," he wrote. "For different reasons, in different ways and to different degrees, companies like Apple, Nike, Disney, Google, Whole Foods, Costco and even UPS strike me as examples of large companies that are well-liked by their customers." On the other end of spectrum, he added, companies like Walmart, Microsoft, Goldman Sachs, and ExxonMobil tended to be feared.

Bezos postulated that this second set of companies was viewed, perhaps unfairly, as engaging in exploitative behavior. He wondered why Microsoft's large base of users had never come out in any significant way to defend the company against its critics and speculated that perhaps customers were simply not satisfied with its products. He theorized that UPS, though not particularly inventive, was blessed by having the unsympathetic U.S. Postal Service as a competitor; Walmart had to deal with a "plethora of sympathetic competitors" in the small downtown stores that competed with it.

But Bezos was dissatisfied with that simplistic conclusion and applied his usual analytical sensibility to parse out why some companies were loved and others feared.

Rudeness is not cool.
Defeating tiny guys is not cool.
Close-following is not cool.
Young is cool.
Risk taking is cool.
Winning is cool.
Polite is cool.
Defeating bigger, unsympathetic guys is cool.
Inventing is cool.
Explorers are cool.
Conquerors are not cool.
Obsessing over competitors is not cool.
Empowering others is cool.
Capturing all the value only for the company is not cool.
Leadership is cool.
Conviction is cool.
Straightforwardness is cool.
Pandering to the crowd is not cool.
Hypocrisy is not cool.
Authenticity is cool.
Thinking big is cool.
The unexpected is cool.
Missionaries are cool.
Mercenaries are not cool.

On an attached spreadsheet, Bezos listed seventeen attributes, including *polite, reliable, risk taking,* and *thinks big,* and he ranked a dozen companies on each particular characteristic. His methodology was highly subjective, he conceded, but his conclusions, laid out at the end of the Amazon.love memo, were aimed at increasing Amazon's odds of standing out among the loved companies. Being polite and reliable or customer-obsessed was not sufficient. Being perceived as inventive, as an explorer rather than a conqueror, was critically important. "I actually believe the four 'unloved' companies are inventive as a matter of substance. But they are not perceived as inventors and pioneers. It is not enough to be inventive—that pioneering spirit must also come across and be perceivable by the customer base," he wrote.

"I propose that one outcome from this offsite could be to assign a more thorough analysis of this topic to a thoughtful VP," Bezos concluded. "We may be able to find actionable tasks that will increase our odds of being a stand out in that first group of companies. Sounds worthy to me!"

CHAPTER 11

The Kingdom of the Question Mark

As it neared its twentieth anniversary, Amazon had finally come to embody the original vision of the everything store, conceived so long ago by Jeff Bezos and David Shaw and set into motion by Bezos and Shel Kaphan. It sold millions of products both new and used and was continually expanding into new product areas; industrial supplies, high-end apparel, art, and wine were among the new categories introduced in 2012 and 2013. It hosted the storefronts of thousands of other retailers in its bustling Marketplace and the computer infrastructure of thousands of other technology companies, universities, and government labs, part of its flourishing Web Services business. Clearly Jeff Bezos believed there were no limits to the company's mission and to the variety of products that could be sold on the Internet.

If you were to search the world for the polar opposite of this sprawling conglomerate, a store that cultivated not massive selection but an exclusive assortment of high-end products and thrived not on brand loyalty but on the amiable personality of its proprietor, you might just settle on a small bike shop north of Phoenix, in Glendale, Arizona. It's called the Roadrunner Bike Center.

This somewhat grandiosely named establishment sits in a shoe-box-shaped space in an otherwise ordinary shopping center next to

the Hot Cutz Spa and Salon and down a ways from a Walmart grocery store. It offers a small selection of premium BMX and dirt
bikes from companies like Giant, Haro, and Redline, brands that
carefully select their retail partners and generally do not sell to websites or discount outlets. Many customers have patronized this store
for years, even though it has moved three times within the Phoenix
area.

"The old guy that runs this is always there and you can tell he
loves to fix and sell bikes," writes one customer in a typically favor-
able online review of the store. "When you buy from him he will
take care of you. He also is the cheapest place I have ever taken a
bike for a service, I think sometimes he runs a special for $30! That's
insane!"

A red poster board with the hand-scrawled words *Layaway for
the holidays!* leans against an outside window of the store. It is no
different than any mom-and-pop shop anywhere in the world that's
been carefully tended and nurtured by its owner over the course of
thirty years. Except in this case, the store offers more than just a
strong contrast to Amazon, and the evidence hangs inside, under
the fluorescent lights, next to the front counter. Framed on the wall
is a laminated old newspaper clipping with a photograph of a six-
teen-year-old boy sporting a flattop haircut and standing up on the
pedals of his unicycle, with one hand on the seat and the other
flared daringly out to the side.

I found Ted Jorgensen, Jeff Bezos's biological father, behind the
counter of his store in late 2012. I had considered a number of ways
he might react to my unannounced appearance, but I gave a very
low probability to the likelihood of what actually happened: Jorgensen didn't know who Jeff Bezos was or anything at all about a
company named Amazon.com. He was utterly confused by what I
was telling him and denied being the father of a famous CEO who
was one of the wealthiest men in the world.

But then, when I mentioned the names Jacklyn Gise and Jeffrey, the son they had during their brief teenage marriage, the old man's face flushed with recognition and sadness. "Is he still alive?" he asked, not yet fully comprehending.

"Your son is one of the most successful men on the planet," I told him. I pulled up some photographs of Bezos from the Internet, and, incredibly, for the first time in forty-five years, Jorgensen saw his biological son, and his eyes filled with emotion and disbelief.

I took Jorgensen and his wife, Linda, to dinner that night at a local steakhouse, and his story tumbled out. When the Bezos family moved from Albuquerque to Houston back in 1968, Jorgensen promised Jackie and her father that he would stay out of their lives. He remained in Albuquerque, performing with his troupe, the Unicycle Wranglers, and taking odd jobs. He drove an ambulance and worked as an installer for Western Electric, a local utility.

In his twenties, he moved to Hollywood to help the Wranglers' manager, Lloyd Smith, start a new bike shop, and then he went to Tucson, looking for work. In 1972 he was mugged outside a convenience store after buying cigarettes. The assailants hit him with a two-by-four and broke his jaw in ten places.

Jorgensen moved to Phoenix in 1974, got remarried, and quit drinking. By that time he had lost touch with his ex-wife and their child and forgotten their new last name. He had no way to contact his son or follow his progress, and he says he felt constrained by his promise not to interfere in their lives.

In 1980, he put together every cent he had and bought the bike shop from its owner, who wanted to get out of the business. He has run the store ever since, moving it several times, eventually to its current location on the northern edge of the Phoenix metropolitan area, adjacent to the New River Mountains. He divorced his second wife and met Linda, his third, at the bike shop. She stood him up on their first date but showed up the next time he asked her out. They've been married for twenty-five years. Linda says they've talked privately about Jeffrey and replayed Ted's youthful mistakes for years.

Jorgensen has no other children; Linda has four sons from a previous marriage, and they are close with their stepfather, but he never divulged to them that he had another child—he says he didn't think there was any point. He felt it was a "dead-end street" and was sure he would never see or hear anything about his son again.

Jorgensen is now sixty-nine; he has heart problems, emphysema, and an aversion to the idea of retirement. "I don't want to sit at home and rot in front of the television," he says. He is endearingly friendly and, his wife says, deeply compassionate. (Bezos strongly resembles his mother, especially around the eyes, but he has his father's nose and ears.) Jorgensen's store is less than thirty miles from four different Amazon fulfillment centers, but if he ever saw Jeff Bezos on television or read an article about Amazon, he didn't make the connection. "I didn't know where he was, if he had a good job or not, or if he was alive or dead," he says. The face of his child, frozen in infancy, has been stuck in his mind for nearly half a century.

Jorgensen says that he always wanted to reconnect with his son—whatever his occupation or station—but he blames himself entirely for the collapse of his first marriage and is ashamed to admit that, all those years ago, he agreed to stay out of his life. "I wasn't a good father or a husband," he says. "It was really all my fault. I don't blame Jackie at all." Regret, that formidable adversary Jeff Bezos worked so hard to outrun, hangs heavily over the life of his biological father.

When I left Jorgensen and his wife after dinner that night, they were wistful and still in shock and had decided that they weren't going to tell Linda's sons. The story seemed too far-fetched.

But a few months later, in early 2013, I got a phone call from the youngest son, Darin Fala, a senior project manager at Honeywell who also lives in Phoenix and who spent his teenage years living with Jorgensen and his mother.

Jorgensen, Fala told me, had called a family meeting the previous Saturday afternoon. ("I bet he's going to tell us he has a son or daughter out there," Fala's wife had guessed.) In dramatic fashion, Jorgensen and Linda explained the unlikely situation.

Fala described the gathering as wrenching and tear-filled. "My wife calls me unemotional because she has never seen me cry," Fala says. "Ted is the same way. Saturday was the most emotion I've ever seen out of him, as far as sadness and regret. It was overwhelming."

Jorgensen had decided he wanted to try to reach out to the Bezos family and reestablish contact, and Fala was helping him craft his letters to Bezos and his mother. They would send those letters via both regular mail and e-mail in February of 2013, and would end up waiting nearly five months for a response. Bezos's silence on the topic of his long-lost biological father is unsurprising: he is far more consumed with pressing forward than looking back.

During the phone call, Fala related a discovery of his own. Curious about Bezos, he had watched several clips on the Internet of the Amazon CEO being interviewed, including one from *The Daily Show with Jon Stewart.* And Fala was startled to hear Bezos's notorious, honking laugh.

It was the same unrestrained guffaw that had once echoed off the walls of Fala's childhood home, though over the past few years it had gradually been inhibited by emphysema. "He has Ted's laugh!" Fala says in disbelief. "It's almost exact."

*   *   *

Bezos undoubtedly received and read Jorgensen's e-mail—colleagues say that, with his personal assistants, he reviews all the messages sent to his widely known e-mail address, jeff@amazon.com. In fact, many of the more infamous episodes inside Amazon began with unsolicited e-mails from customers that Bezos forwarded to the relevant executives or employees, adding only a question mark at the top of the message. To the recipients of these e-mails, that notation has the effect of a ticking time bomb.

Within Amazon, an official system ranks the severity of its internal emergencies. A Sev-5 is a relatively inconsequential technical problem that can be solved by engineers in the course of the workday. A Sev-1 is an urgent problem that sets off a cavalcade of pagers (Amazon still gives them to many engineers). It requires an immediate response, and the entire situation will later be reviewed by a member of Bezos's management council, the S Team.

Then there's an entirely separate kind of crisis, what some employees have informally dubbed the Sev-B. That's when an e-mail containing the notorious question mark arrives directly from Bezos. When Amazon employees receive one of these missives, they drop everything they are doing and fling themselves at whatever issue the CEO is highlighting. They've typically got a few hours to solve the problem and prepare a thorough explanation for how it occurred in the first place, a response that will be reviewed by a succession of managers before the answer is presented to Bezos himself. The question mark e-mails, often called escalations, are Bezos's way to ensure that potential problems are addressed and that the customer's voice is always heard inside Amazon.

One of the more memorable recent episodes at Amazon began with such an escalation in late 2010. It had come to Bezos's attention that customers who browsed — but didn't buy — in the lubricant section of Amazon's sexual-wellness category were receiving personalized e-mails promoting a variety of gels and other intimacy facilitators. Even though the extent of Bezos's communication to his marketing staff consisted of a single piece of punctuation, they could tell — he was pissed off. Bezos believed the marketing department's e-mails caused customers embarrassment and should not have been sent.

Bezos likes to say that when he's angry, "just wait five minutes," and the mood will pass like a tropical squall.[1] When it comes to issues of bungled customer service, though, that is rarely true. The e-mail marketing team knew the topic was delicate and nervously prepared an explanation. Amazon's direct-marketing tool was decentralized, and category managers could generate e-mail campaigns to customers who had looked at certain product categories but did not make purchases. Such e-mails tended to tip vacillating shoppers into buying and were responsible for hundreds of millions of dollars in Amazon's annual sales. In the case of the lubricant e-mail, though, a low-level product manager had clearly overstepped the bounds of propriety. But the marketing team never got to send this explanation. Bezos was demanding a meeting to discuss the issue.

On a weekday morning, Jeff Wilke, Doug Herrington, Steven Shure (the vice president of worldwide marketing and a former executive at Time Inc.), and several other employees gathered and waited solemnly in a conference room. Bezos glided in briskly. He started the meeting with his customary "Hello, everybody," and followed that with "So, Steve Shure is sending out e-mails about lubricants."

Bezos didn't sit down. He locked eyes with Shure. He was clearly fuming. "I want you to shut down the channel," he said. "We can build a one-hundred-billion-dollar company without sending out a single fucking e-mail."

There was an animated argument. Amazon's culture is notoriously confrontational, and it begins with Bezos, who believes that truth springs forth when ideas and perspectives are banged against each other, sometimes violently. In the ensuing scrum, Wilke and his colleagues argued that lubricants were available in grocery stores and drugstores and were not, technically, that embarrassing. They also pointed out that Amazon generated a significant volume of sales with such e-mails. Bezos didn't care; no amount of revenue was worth jeopardizing customer trust. It was a revealing—and confirming—moment. He was willing to slay a profitable aspect of his business rather than test Amazon's bond with its customers. "Who in this room needs to get up and shut down the channel?" he snapped.

Eventually, they compromised. E-mail marketing for certain categories such as health and personal care was terminated altogether. The company also decided to build a central filtering tool to ensure that category managers could no longer promote sensitive products, so matters of etiquette were not subject to personal taste. E-mail marketing lived to fight another day.

The story highlighted one of the contradictions of life inside

Amazon. Long past the era of using the editorial judgment of employees to drive changes to the website, the company relies on metrics to make almost every important decision, such as what features to introduce or kill. Yet random customer anecdotes, the opposite of cold, hard data, also carry tremendous weight and can change Amazon policy. If one customer has a bad experience, Bezos often assumes it reflects a larger problem and escalates the resolution of the matter inside his company with a question mark.

Many Amazon employees are all too familiar with these fire drills and find them disruptive. "Why are entire teams required to drop everything on a dime to respond to a question mark escalation?" an employee once asked at one of the company's all-hands meetings, which by 2011 were being held in Seattle's KeyArena, a basketball coliseum with more than seventeen thousand seats.

"Every anecdote from a customer matters," Jeff Wilke answered. "We research each of them because they tell us something about our metrics and processes. It's an audit that is done for us by our customers. We treat them as precious sources of information."

Amazon styles itself as highly decentralized and promises that new employees can make decisions independently. But Bezos is capable of stopping any process dead in its tracks if it creates a problem for even a single customer. In the twelve months after the lube crisis, Bezos made it his personal mission to clean up the e-mail channel. Employees of that department suddenly found themselves in the hottest possible spot at Amazon: under the withering eye of the founder himself.

Despite the scars and occasional bouts of post-traumatic stress disorder, former Amazon employees often consider their time at the company the most productive of their careers. Their colleagues were smart, the work was challenging, and frequent lateral movement between departments offered constant opportunities for learning. "Everybody knows how hard it is and chooses to be there," says Faisal Masud, who spent five years in the retail business. "You are learning constantly and the pace of innovation is thrilling. I filed patents; I innovated. There is a fierce competitiveness in everything you do."

But some also express anguish about their experience. Bezos says the company attracts a certain kind of person who likes to pioneer and invent, but former employees frequently complain that Amazon has the bureaucracy of a big company with the infrastructure and pace of a startup, with lots of duplicate efforts and poor communication that makes it difficult to get things done. The people who do well at Amazon are often those who thrive in an adversarial atmosphere with almost constant friction. Bezos abhors what he calls "social cohesion," the natural impulse to seek consensus. He'd rather his minions battled it out in arguments backed by numbers and passion, and he has codified this approach in one of Amazon's fourteen leadership principles—the company's highly prized values that are often discussed and inculcated into new hires.[2]

Have Backbone; Disagree and Commit

Leaders are obligated to respectfully challenge decisions when they disagree, even when doing so is uncomfortable or exhausting. Leaders have conviction and are tenacious. They do not compromise for the sake of social cohesion. Once a decision is determined, they commit wholly.

Some employees love this confrontational culture and find they can't work effectively anywhere else. The professional networking site LinkedIn is full of executives who left Amazon and then returned. Inside the company, this is referred to as a boomerang.

But other escapees call Amazon's internal environment a "gladiator culture" and wouldn't think of returning. There are many who last less than two years. "It's a weird mix of a startup that is trying to be super corporate and a corporation that is trying hard to still be a startup," says Jenny Dibble, who spent five months there as a marketing manager in 2011, trying, ineffectively, to get the company to use more social-media tools. She found her bosses were not particularly receptive to her ideas and that the long hours were incompatible with raising a family. "It was not a friendly environment," she says.

Even leaving Amazon can be a combative process—the company is not above sending letters threatening legal action if an employee takes a similar job at a competitor. It's more evidence of that "fierce competitiveness" mentioned by Faisal Masud, who left Amazon for eBay in 2010 and received such a legal threat (eBay settled the matter privately). This perpetual exodus of employees hardly seems to hurt Amazon, though. The company, aided by the appeal of its steadily increasing stock price, has become an accomplished recruiter of new talent. In 2012 alone, Amazon's ranks swelled to 88,400 full-time and part-time time employees, up 57 percent from the year before.

The compensation packages at Amazon are designed to minimize the cost to the company and maximize the chances that employees will stick around through the predictable adversity that comes with joining the firm. New hires are given an industry-average base salary, a signing bonus spread over two years, and a grant of restricted stock units over four years. But unlike other technology companies, such as Google and Microsoft, which spread out their stock grants evenly, Amazon backloads the grant toward the end of the four-year period. Employees typically get 5 percent of their shares at the end of their first year, 15 percent their second year, and then 20 percent every six months over the final two years. Ensuing grants vest over two years and are also backloaded, to ensure that employees keep working hard and are never inclined to coast.

Managers in departments of fifty people or more are required to "top-grade" their subordinates along a curve and must dismiss the least effective performers. As a result of this ongoing examination, many Amazon employees live in perpetual fear. A common experience among Amazon workers is a feeling of genuine surprise when one receives a good performance review. Managers are so parsimonious with compliments that underlings tend to spend their days anticipating their termination.

There is little in the way of perks or unexpected performance bonuses at Amazon, though it has come along since the 1990s, when Bezos refused that early suggestion to give employees bus passes because he didn't want them to feel pressure to leave at a reasonable hour. Employees now get ORCA cards that entitle them to free rides on Seattle's regional transit system. Parking at the company's offices in South Lake Union costs $220 a month and Amazon reimburses employees — for $180.

Still, evidence of the company's constitutional frugality is everywhere. Conference-room tables are a collection of blond-wood door-desks shoved together side by side. The vending machines take credit cards, and food in the company cafeterias is not subsidized. When a new hire joins the company, he gets a backpack with a power adapter, a laptop dock, and some orientation materials. When someone resigns, he is asked to hand in all that equipment — including the backpack. The company is constantly searching for ways to reduce costs and pass on those savings to customers in the form of lower prices. This also is embedded in the sacrosanct leadership principles:

Frugality

We try not to spend money on things that don't matter to customers. Frugality breeds resourcefulness, self-sufficiency and invention. There are no extra points for headcount, budget size or fixed expense.

All of this comes from Bezos himself. Amazon's values are his business principles, molded through two decades of surviving in the thin atmosphere of low profit margins and fierce skepticism from the outside world. In a way, the entire company is scaffolding built around his brain — an amplification machine meant to disseminate his ingenuity and drive across the greatest possible radius. "It's scaffolding to magnify the thinking embodied by Jeff, to the greatest extent possible," says Jeff Wilke when I bounce that theory off him. "Jeff was learning as he went along. He learned things from each of us who had expertise and incorporated the best pieces into his mental model. Now everyone is expected to think as much as they can like Jeff."

Bezos's top executives are always modeling Bezos-like behavior. In the fall of 2012, I had dinner with Diego Piacentini at La Spiga, his favorite Italian restaurant in Seattle's Capitol Hill neighborhood. He graciously insisted on picking up the tab, and after paying, he almost theatrically tore up the receipt. "The company is not paying for this," he said.

The rhythms of Amazon are the rhythms of Bezos, and its customs are closely tuned to how he prefers to process information and maximize his time. He personally runs the biannual operating review periods for the entire company, dubbed OP1 (done over the summer) and OP2 (done after the holiday season). Teams work intensely for months preparing for these sessions, drawing up six-page documents that spell out their plans for the year ahead. A few years ago, the company refined this process further to make the narratives more easily digestible for Bezos and other S Team members, who cycle through many topics during these reviews. Now every document includes at the top of the page a list of a few rules, called tenets, the principles for each group that guide the hard decisions and allow them all to move fast, without constant supervision.

Bezos is like a chess master playing countless games simultaneously, with the boards organized in such a way that he can efficiently tend to each match.

Some of these chess games get more attention than others. Bezos spends more time on Amazon's newer businesses, such as Amazon Web Services, the company's streaming-video initiative, and, in particular, the Kindle and Kindle Fire efforts. ("I don't think you can even fart in the Kindle building without Jeff's approval," quipped one longtime executive.) In these divisions, stress levels are high and any semblance of balance between work and home falls by the wayside.

Once a week, usually on Tuesday, various departments at Amazon meet with their managers to review long spreadsheets of the data important to their business. Customer anecdotes have no place at these meetings. The numbers alone are a proxy for what is working and what is broken, how customers are behaving, and, ultimately, how well the company overall is performing.

The meetings can be intense and intimidating. "This is what, for employees, is so absolutely scary and impressive about the executive team. They force you to look at the numbers and answer every single question about why specific things happened," says Dave Cotter, who spent four years at Amazon as a general manager in various divisions. "Because Amazon has so much volume, it's a way to make very quick decisions and not get into subjective debates. The data doesn't lie."

The metrics meetings culminate with the weekly business review every Wednesday, one of the most important rituals at Amazon, run by Wilke. Sixty managers in the retail business gather in one room to review their departments, share data about defects and inventory turns, and talk about forecasts and the complex interactions among different parts of the company.

Bezos does not attend these meetings. But he can always make his presence felt anywhere in the company. After the lubricant crisis, for example, e-mail marketing fell squarely under his purview. He carefully monitored efforts to filter the kinds of messages that could be sent to customers and he tried to think about the challenge of e-mail outreach in fresh ways. Then, in late 2011, he had what he considered to be a significant new idea.

Bezos is a fan of e-mail newsletters such as VSL.com, a daily assortment of cultural tidbits from the Web, and Cool Tools, a compendium of technology tips and product reviews written by Kevin Kelly, a founding editor of *Wired*. Both e-mails are short, well written, and informative. Perhaps, Bezos reasoned, Amazon should be sending a single well-crafted e-mail every week — a short digital magazine — instead of a succession of bland, algorithm-generated marketing pitches. He asked marketing vice president Steve Shure to explore the idea.

Shure formed a team and they spent two months coming up with trial concepts. Bezos gave them little direction, but their broad mandate was to create an entirely new type of e-mail for customers—the kind of personal voice that Amazon had lost more than ten years ago, when it downsized its editorial division after the acrimonious intramural competition with P13N and Amabot.

From late 2011 through early 2012, Shure's group presented a variety of concepts to Bezos, including one that revolved around celebrity Q and As and another that highlighted interesting historical facts about products on the site. The project never progressed—it fared poorly in tests with customers—but several participants remember the process as being particularly excruciating. In one meeting, Bezos quietly thumbed through the mockups, styled in the customary Amazon format of a press release, as everyone waited in tense, edge-of-the-seat silence. Then he tore the documents apart. "Here's the problem with this, I'm already bored," he said. He seemed to like the last concept the most, which suggested profiling a selection of products on the site that were suddenly hot, like Guy Fawkes masks and CDs by the Grammy-winning British singer Adele. "But the headlines need to be punchier," he told the group, which included the writers of the material. "And some of this is just bad writing. If you were doing this as a blogger, you would starve."

Finally he turned his attention to Shure, the marketing vice president, who, like so many other marketing vice presidents throughout the company's history, was a frequent target.

"Steve, why haven't I seen anything on this in three months?"

"Well, I had to find an editor and work through mockups."

"This is developing too slow. Do you care about this?"

"Yes, Jeff, we care."

"Strip the design down, it's too complicated. Also, it needs to move faster!"

Faster was one way to describe 2012 and the first half of 2013. Over those months, Amazon's stock rose 60 percent. The company issued a total of 237 press releases—an average of 1.6 announcements for every two weekdays. Since the company was now beginning to collect sales tax in many states, it didn't have to sidestep nexus issues and so opened more than a dozen new fulfillment and customer-service centers around the world. It acquired Kiva Systems, a Boston company building mobile robots meant to one day replace the human pickers in fulfillment centers, for $775 million in cash. It renewed its push into apparel with its dedicated website MyHabit.com and opened a new store for industrial and scientific equipment, Amazon Supply.

Amazon also expanded a service that allowed advertisers to reach Amazon customers on all of the company's websites and devices. Run by business-development chief Jeff Blackburn, advertising at Amazon is a highly profitable side business that helps subsidize free shipping and low prices and funds some of the company's expensive long-term projects, like building its own hardware.

To distinguish its growing digital ecosystem from rival platforms offered by Apple and Google, Amazon spent millions to acquire and create new movies and television shows to add to its free Prime Instant Video catalog, and through Amazon's publishing divisions, it funded the publication of many exclusive books for the Kindle. Amazon's chief rivals, Apple and Google, are arguably better positioned in this burgeoning digital world and have considerably greater resources. So Bezos is hedging his bets; if customers choose Apple iPads or Google tablets, they can still shop on Amazon and play their music collections and read their Kindle books on a variety of applications that have been rolled out for its rivals' devices.

In the fall of 2012, hundreds of journalists turned out at an airplane hangar in Santa Monica to watch Bezos unveil a new line of Kindle Fire tablets, including an iPad-size jumbo version and the $119 Kindle Paperwhite, a dedicated e-reader with a glowing, front-lit screen. "This achieves our original vision," Bezos told me in an interview after the event, referring to the latest dedicated reading device. "I'm sure we'll figure out ways to continue forward, but this is a step-change product."

Earlier that same week, a federal judge had approved a settlement with three of the major book publishers in the Justice Department's antitrust case over agency pricing. (The other two publishers targeted in the investigation would settle within the next few months.) Amazon was now free to resume discounting new and bestselling e-books. I asked Bezos about it but he didn't care to gloat. "We are excited to be allowed to lower prices" was all he said.

In December, Amazon held its first conference for customers of Amazon Web Services at the Sands Expo Center in Las Vegas. Six thousand developers showed up and listened intently as AWS executives Andy Jassy and Werner Vogels discussed the future of cloud computing. The size and passion of the crowd was an emphatic validation of Amazon's unlikely emergence as a pioneer in the field of enterprise computing. On the second day of the conference, Bezos himself took the stage and in a freewheeling discussion with Vogels gave a rare window into his personal projects, like the Clock of the Long Now, that mechanical timepiece designed to last for millennia that engineers are preparing to build inside a remote mountain on Bezos's ranch in Texas. "The symbol is important for a couple of reasons. If [humans] think long term, we can accomplish things that we wouldn't otherwise accomplish," Bezos said. "Time horizons matter, they matter a lot. The other thing I would point out is that we humans are getting awfully sophisticated in technological ways and have a lot of potential to be very dangerous to ourselves. It seems to me that we, as a species, have to start thinking longer term. So this is a symbol. I think symbols can be very powerful."

On the stage, Bezos then predictably unleashed a steady tide of Jeffisms, about long-term thinking, about a willingness to fail and to be misunderstood, and about that shocking revelation so many years ago, in the very first SoDo warehouse, that it might be a great idea to add —*He's not really going to tell that story again, is he?*— packing tables!

The packing-table anecdote may be showing its age, but Bezos is trying to reinforce the same values. Like the late Steve Jobs, Bezos has gradually worn down employees, investors, and a skeptical public and turned them toward his way of thinking. Any process can be improved. Defects that are invisible to the knowledgeable may be obvious to newcomers. The simplest solutions are the best. Repeating all these anecdotes isn't rote monotony — it's calculated strategy. "The rest of us try to muddle around with complicated contradictory goals and it makes it harder for people to help us," says his friend Danny Hillis. "Jeff is very clear and simple about his goals, and the way he articulates them makes it easy for others, because it's consistent.

"If you look at why Amazon is so different than almost any other company that started early on the Internet, it's because Jeff approached it from the very beginning with that long-term vision," Hillis continues. "It was a multidecade project. The notion that he can accomplish a huge amount with a larger time frame, if he is steady about it, is fundamentally his philosophy."

*　　*　　*

By 2012, Amazon had completed its move to its new office buildings in Seattle's South Lake Union district. Another transition occurred at around this same time, though it was evident only to employees at first. In signs around the new campus, and on the rare tchotchkes like mugs and T-shirts that were available to employees after the move, the company's name was represented as simply Amazon, not Amazon.com. For years Bezos had been adamant about using the longer version, part of an effort to engrave the Web address on customers' minds. Now the company produced so many things, including cloud services and hardware, that the anachronistic original moniker no longer made sense. The name on the website was abbreviated in March of 2012. Few people noticed.

Amazon, it seemed, was a company in constant flux. Yet some things remained the same. On a cold, wet Tuesday morning in early November 2012 at around nine o'clock, a Honda minivan pulled up to Day One North, on the corner of Terry Avenue and Republican Street in Seattle's South Lake Union neighborhood. Jeff Bezos, sitting in the passenger seat, leaned over to kiss his wife, MacKenzie, good-bye, got out of the car, and walked self-assuredly into the building to start another day.

In many ways, Bezos's life has become as complicated as Lee Scott's was back in 2000 when Bezos visited the former Walmart CEO and marveled at the security around him. Bezos may not get ferried to work in a black sedan, but Amazon still spends $1.6 million per year on personal security for him and his family, according to the company's financial reports.

His small domestic scene with MacKenzie speaks to at least one normal routine he has managed to preserve amid the unimaginable complexity that comes with Amazon's towering success. The family can hire drivers; they can buy limousines and private airplanes. Yet they still own a modest Honda, albeit a larger model than the Accord of a decade ago, and MacKenzie often delivers their four children to school and then drives her husband to work.

There is nothing modest about their wealth, of course. Bezos's fortune is now estimated at $25 billion, making him the twelfth-richest person in the United States.[3]

The family is exceedingly private, yet their lives cannot be completely hidden from view. Their lakefront mansion in the wealthy residential enclave of Medina, near the home of Bill and Melinda Gates, was renovated in 2010 and sits on 5.35 acres. It has 29,000 square feet of living space across two buildings, according to public records, and that's not including a caretaker's cottage and a boathouse — the site where Bezos first organized the team that would build Amazon Prime.[4]

In addition to the primary residence, the Bezos family owns homes in Aspen, Beverly Hills, and New York City, plus the sprawling 290,000-acre ranch in Texas, where Blue Origin has a facility and where its rockets will begin their trips to space. MacKenzie rents a one-bedroom apartment near their home in Medina that she uses as a private office to write. She is the author of two novels, including *Traps,* published in 2012. "I am definitely a lottery winner of a certain kind," she told *Vogue* magazine in a rare profile in 2012, referring to her husband's success. "It makes my life wonderful in many ways, but that's not the lottery I feel defined by. The fact that

I got wonderful parents who believed in education and never doubted I could be a writer, the fact that I have a spouse I love, those are the things that define me."[5]

Bezos and MacKenzie seem to share the skill of efficiently dispersing their time across many personal responsibilities and multiple projects. For Bezos, in addition to his family and Amazon, there's Blue Origin, where he typically spends each Wednesday, and Bezos Expeditions, his personal venture-capital firm, which holds stakes in companies such as Twitter, the taxi service Uber, the news site Business Insider, and the robot firm Rethink Robotics. Since August of 2013, Bezos has owned the *Washington Post* newspaper and has said he wants to apply his passion for invention and experimentation to reviving the storied newspaper. "He invests in things where information technology can disrupt existing models," says Rodney Brooks, the MIT robotics professor behind Rethink Robotics, which aims to put inexpensive robots on manufacturing assembly lines. "He's certainly not hands-on but he has been a good person to talk to when various conundrums come up. When we go ask him questions, it's worth listening to his answers."

Bezos coordinates closely with the creators of the Clock of the Long Now and oversees its quarterly review sessions, which the clock engineers call Ticks. "He's hell on the details and in the thick of the design and very strict on where costs are going," says Stewart Brand, the cochairman of the Long Now Foundation.

Bezos and MacKenzie are personally involved in the Bezos Family Foundation, which doles out education grants and mobilizes students to help other young people in impoverished countries and disaster zones. The foundation is run by Jackie and Mike Bezos, and Christina Bezos Poore and Mark Bezos, Jeff's siblings, are directors. The family has imported a little Amazon-style management to their philanthropy. In the main conference room of the foundation's office, a few blocks from Amazon's headquarters, is a rag doll that they often prop up in an empty chair during meetings. The doll is meant to represent the student they are trying to help — just as Bezos once had a habit of keeping a chair empty in meetings to represent the customer.

The Bezos family is unusually close-knit and focused on the future. But occasionally the past does catch up with them. In June 2013, on a Wednesday evening close to midnight, Jeff Bezos finally responded to the messages sent by Ted Jorgensen, his biological father. In a short but heartfelt e-mail, sent to Jorgensen's stepson because Jorgensen himself does not use the Internet, Bezos tried to put the old man at ease. He wrote that he empathized with the impossibly difficult choices that his teenage parents were forced to make and said that he had enjoyed a happy childhood nonetheless. He said that he harbored no ill will toward Jorgensen at all, and he asked him to cast aside any lingering regret over the circumstances of their lives. And then he wished his long-lost biological father the very best.

*   *   *

When you have fit yourself snugly into Jeff Bezos's worldview and then evaluated both the successes and failures of Amazon over the past two decades, the future of the company becomes easy to predict. The answer to almost every conceivable question is yes.

Will Amazon move to free next-day and same-day delivery for Prime members? Yes, eventually, when Amazon has so many customers in each urban area that placing a fulfillment center right outside every city becomes practical. Bezos's goal is and always has been to take all the inconvenience out of online shopping and deliver products and services to customers in the most efficient manner possible.

Will Amazon one day own its own delivery trucks? Yes, eventually, because controlling the so-called last-mile delivery to its customers can help fulfill that vision and improve the company's ability to meet the precise delivery promises it relishes making to customers.

Will Amazon roll out its grocery service, Amazon Fresh, beyond Seattle and parts of Los Angeles and San Francisco? Yes, when it has perfected the mechanics of profitable storage and delivery of perishables, like vegetables and fruit. Bezos does not believe Amazon can grow to the scale of Walmart without mastering the science of groceries and apparel.

Will Amazon introduce a mobile phone or an Internet-connected television set-top box? Yes (and possibly before this book is published), because the company wants to offer its services on all the connected devices that its customers use without having to rely entirely on the hardware of its chief competitors.

Will Amazon expand beyond the ten countries where it currently operates retail websites? Yes, eventually. Bezos's long-term goal is to sell everything, everywhere. As Russia, for example, develops a stronger shipping infrastructure and a more reliable credit card processing system, Amazon will introduce its e-commerce store and digital services there, perhaps by acquiring local companies or by seeding the market with the Kindle and Kindle Fire, as it did in Brazil in 2012 and in India in 2013.

Will Amazon always buy its products from manufacturers? No; at some point it might *print* them right in its fulfillment centers. The evolving technology known as 3-D printing, in which microwave-size machines extrude plastic material to create objects based on digital models, is just the kind of disruptive revolution that fascinates Bezos and could allow him to eliminate more costs from the supply chain. In 2013, Amazon took the first step into this world, opening a site for 3-D printers and supplies.

Will antitrust authorities eventually come to scrutinize Amazon and its market power? Yes, I believe that is likely, because the company is growing increasingly monolithic in markets like books and electronics, and rivals have fallen by the wayside. But as we have seen with the disputes over sales tax and e-book pricing, Amazon is a masterly navigator of the law and is careful to stay on the right side of it. Like Google, it benefits from the example of Microsoft's antitrust debacle in the 1990s, which provided a powerful object lesson of how aggressive monopolistic behavior can nearly ruin a company.

These are not fever dreams. They are near inevitabilities. It's an easy prediction to make—that Jeff Bezos will do what he has always done. He will attempt to move faster, work his employees harder, make bolder bets, and pursue both big inventions and small ones, all to achieve his grand vision for Amazon — that it be not just an everything store, but ultimately an everything company.

Amazon may be the most beguiling company that ever existed, and it is just getting started. It is both missionary *and* mercenary, and throughout the history of business and other human affairs, that has always been a potent combination. "We don't have a single big advantage," he once told an old adversary, publisher Tim O'Reilly, back when they were arguing over Amazon protecting its patented 1-Click ordering method from rivals like Barnes & Noble. "So we have to weave a rope of many small advantages."

Amazon is still weaving that rope. That is its future, to keep weaving and growing, manifesting the constitutional relentlessness of its founder and his vision. And it will continue to expand until either Jeff Bezos exits the scene or no one is left to stand in his way.

Acknowledgments

For years I talked about writing a book about Amazon. And that's probably what I'd still be doing — talking — if it weren't for the help and support of my wonderful friends, family, and colleagues.

Two years ago, my agent Pilar Queen gently instructed me to stop procrastinating and deliver a book proposal. She then became a tenacious champion for this project. At Little, Brown, executive editor John Parsley gave this book the kind of careful editorial attention that is supposedly going out of style at traditional publishers, at least according to certain critics of the book business. Additional thanks go to Reagan Arthur, Michael Pietsch, Geoff Shandler, Nicole Dewey, Fiona Brown, Pamela Marshall, Tracy Roe, and Malin von Euler-Hogan at Little, Brown for steering this book through the birthing process with professionalism and enthusiasm.

I owe an enormous debt to Craig Berman and Drew Herdener in Amazon's public-relations department. While they were always stubborn advocates for the company, they also saw the need for, and perhaps the inevitability of, a definitive book-length look at Amazon's remarkable rise. I'm grateful to Jeff Wilke, Diego Piacentini, Andy Jassy, Russ Grandinetti, Jeff Blackburn, and Steve Kessel at Amazon, who all took the time to talk to me, and of course to Jeff

Bezos, for approving innumerable interviews with his friends, family, and employees.

Over the course of 2012 and 2013, I spent considerable time in Seattle, and a few families there made me feel especially welcome. Nick and Emily Wingfield put me up in their cozy spare bedroom, and I got to play Trivial Pursuit *Star Wars* over breakfast with their wonderful kids, Beatrice and Miller. Scott Pinizzotto and Ali Frank were great hosts on several occasions.

In Silicon Valley, Jill Hazelbaker, Shernaz Daver, Dani Dudeck, Andrew Kovacs, Christina Lee, Tiffany Spencer, Chris Prouty, and Margit Wennmachers provided helpful connections. Susan Prosser at DomainTools helped me to scour the domain-name archives for the early alternatives to Amazon.com. My old Columbia classmate Charles Ardai gave me a head start on untangling the long-ago D. E. Shaw days. Like so many other journalists trying to decipher the modern enigma that is Amazon, I relied heavily on the wisdom of Scott Devitt of Morgan Stanley, Scot Wingo of ChannelAdvisor, and Fiona Dias of ShopRunner.

At *Bloomberg Businessweek,* I've found a comfortable home that not only offers a great platform for serious business journalism but also accommodates ambitious projects like this one. Josh Tyrangiel, Brad Wieners, Romesh Ratnesar, Ellen Pollock, and Norman Pearlstine gave me incredible support and leeway to write this book. My editor Jim Aley provided a careful first read. Diana Suryakusuma helped me assemble the photographs under a tight deadline. My friend and colleague Ashlee Vance proved an invaluable sounding board when I needed to discuss the thornier challenges of telling this story.

I also want to thank fellow journalists Steven Levy, Ethan Watters, Adam Rogers, George Anders, Dan McGinn, Nick Bilton, Claire Cain Miller, Damon Darlin, John Markoff, Jim Brunner, Alan Deutschman, Tom Giles, Doug MacMillan, Adam Satariano, Motoko Rich, and Peter Burrows. Nick Sanchez provided stellar research and reporting assistance for this book, and Morgan Mason from the journalism program at the University of Nevada at Reno assisted with interviews of Amazon associates at the fulfillment center in Fernley, Nevada.

My family was remarkably helpful and patient throughout this process, particularly in taking up the slack when I disappeared into reporting and writing. My parents Robert Stone and Carol Glick have always been wonderfully supportive and nurturing. Josh Krafchin, Miriam Stone, Dave Stone, Monica Stone, Jon Stone, and Steve Stone were great sounding boards. My brothers, Brian Stone and Eric Stone, and Becca Zoller Stone, Luanne Stone, and Jennifer Granick were awesome, as always.

While they were only vaguely aware of a distraction they called "Daddy's book," my twin daughters, Calista and Isabella Stone, provided the motivation behind this work. My hope and belief is that it will remain relevant history when they are old enough to find it interesting.

And I couldn't have made it across the finish line without the loving support of Tiffany Fox.

Appendix

Jeff's Reading List

Books have nurtured Amazon since its creation and shaped its culture and strategy. Here are a dozen books widely read by executives and employees that are integral to understanding the company.

The Remains of the Day, by Kazuo Ishiguro (1989).

Jeff Bezos's favorite novel, about a butler who wistfully recalls his career in service during wartime Great Britain. Bezos has said he learns more from novels than nonfiction.

Sam Walton: Made in America, by Sam Walton with John Huey (1992).

In his autobiography, Walmart's founder expounds on the principles of discount retailing and discusses his core values of frugality and a bias for action — a willingness to try a lot of things and make many mistakes. Bezos included both in Amazon's corporate values.

Memos from the Chairman, by Alan Greenberg (1996).

A collection of memos to employees by the chairman of the now-defunct investment bank Bear Stearns. In his memos, Greenberg is constantly restating the bank's core values, especially modesty and frugality. His repetition of wisdom from a fictional philosopher presages Amazon's annual recycling of its original 1997 letter to shareholders.

The Mythical Man-Month, by Frederick P. Brooks Jr. (1975).

An influential computer scientist makes the counterintuitive argument that small groups of engineers are more effective than larger ones at handling complex software projects. The book lays out the theory behind Amazon's two-pizza teams.

Built to Last: Successful Habits of Visionary Companies, by Jim Collins and Jerry I. Porras (1994).

The famous management book about why certain companies succeed over time. A core ideology guides these firms, and only those employees who embrace the central mission flourish; others are "expunged like a virus" from the companies.

Good to Great: Why Some Companies Make the Leap . . . and Others Don't, by Jim Collins (2001).

Collins briefed Amazon executives on his seminal management book before its publication. Companies must confront the brutal facts of their business, find out what they are uniquely good at, and master their flywheel, in which each part of the business reinforces and accelerates the other parts.

Creation: Life and How to Make It, by Steve Grand (2001).

A video-game designer argues that intelligent systems can be created from the bottom up if one devises a set of primitive building blocks. The book was influential in the creation of Amazon Web Services, or AWS, the service that popularized the notion of the cloud.

The Innovator's Dilemma: The Revolutionary Book That Will Change the Way You Do Business, by Clayton M. Christensen (1997).

An enormously influential business book whose principles Amazon acted on and that facilitated the creation of the Kindle and AWS. Some companies are reluctant to embrace disruptive technology because it might alienate customers and undermine their core businesses, but Christensen argues that ignoring potential disruption is even costlier.

The Goal: A Process of Ongoing Improvement, by Eliyahu M. Goldratt and Jeff Cox (1984).

An exposition of the science of manufacturing written in the guise of the novel, the book encourages companies to identify the biggest constraints in their operations and then structure their organizations to get the most out of those constraints. *The Goal* was a bible for Jeff Wilke and the team that fixed Amazon's fulfillment network.

Lean Thinking: Banish Waste and Create Wealth in Your Corporation, by James P. Womack and Daniel T. Jones (1996).

The production philosophy pioneered by Toyota calls for a focus on those activities that create value for the customer and the systematic eradication of everything else.

Data-Driven Marketing: The 15 Metrics Everyone in Marketing Should Know, by Mark Jeffery (2010).

A guide to using data to measure everything from customer satisfaction to the effectiveness of marketing. Amazon employees must support all assertions with data, and if the data has a weakness, they must point it out or their colleagues will do it for them.

The Black Swan: The Impact of the Highly Improbable, by Nassim Nicholas Taleb (2007).

The scholar argues that people are wired to see patterns in chaos while remaining blind to unpredictable events, with massive consequences. Experimentation and empiricism trumps the easy and obvious narrative.

Notes

Prologue

1 Jeff Bezos, keynote address at Tepper School of Business graduation, Carnegie Mellon University, May 18, 2008.

Part I
Chapter 1: The House of Quants

1 Jeff Bezos, speech at Lake Forest College, February 26, 1998.
2 Mark Leibovich, *The New Imperialists* (New York: Prentice Hall, 2002), 84.
3 Rebecca Johnson, "MacKenzie Bezos: Writer, Mother of Four, and High-Profile Wife," *Vogue,* February 20, 2013.
4 Eerily, here is how Bezos described the third-market opportunity to *Investment Dealers' Digest* on November 15, 1993: "We wanted something to differentiate our product. We think there is a desire for one stop shopping."
5 Michael Peltz, "The Power of Six," *Institutional Investor* (March 2009). "David Shaw envisioned D. E. Shaw 'as essentially a research lab that happened to invest, and not as a financial firm that happened to have a few people playing with equations.'"
6 Leibovich, *The New Imperialists,* 85.
7 Peter de Jonge, "Riding the Perilous Waters of Amazon.com," *New York Times Magazine,* March 14, 1999.
8 John Quarterman, *Matrix News.*

9 Jeff Bezos interview, Academy of Achievement, May 4, 2001.

10 Jeff Bezos, speech at Lake Forest College, February 26, 1998.

11 Jeff Bezos, speech to Commonwealth Club of California, July 27, 1998.

12 Jeff Bezos, speech to the American Association of Publishers, March 18, 1999.

Chapter 2: The Book of Bezos

1 Robert Spector, *Amazon.com: Get Big Fast* (New York: HarperCollins, 2000). Spector's book offers a comprehensive account of Amazon's early years.

2 Jeff Bezos, speech to the American Association of Publishers, March 18, 1999.

3 David Sheff, "The *Playboy* Interview: Jeff Bezos," *Playboy,* February 1, 2000.

4 Ibid.

5 Adi Ignatius, "Jeff Bezos on Leading for the Long-Term at Amazon," *HBR IdeaCast* (blog), *Harvard Business Review,* January 3, 2013, http://blogs.hbr.org/ideacast/2013/01/jeff-bezos-on-leading-for-the.html.

6 Jeff Bezos, speech to the American Association of Publishers, March 18, 1999.

7 Jeff Bezos, speech at Lake Forest College, February 26, 1998.

8 Ibid.

9 Amazon.com Inc. S-1, filed March 24, 1997.

10 Mukul Pandya and Robbie Shell, eds., "Lasting Leadership: Lessons from the 25 Most Influential Business People of Our Times," Knowledge@Wharton, October 20, 2004, http://knowledge.wharton.upenn.edu/article.cfm?articleid=1054.

11 Ibid.

12 James Marcus, *Amazonia* (New York: New Press, 2004).

13 Jeff Bezos, speech to Commonwealth Club of California, July 27, 1998.

14 Cynthia Mayer, "Investing It; Does Amazon = 2 Barnes & Nobles?," *New York Times,* July 19, 1998.

15 Jeff Bezos, interview by Charlie Rose, *Charlie Rose,* PBS, July 28, 2010.

16 Justin Hibbard, "Wal-Mart v. Amazon.com: The Inside Story," *InformationWeek,* February 22, 1999.

17 Jeff Bezos interview, Academy of Achievement, May 4, 2001.

Chapter 3: Fever Dreams

1 One explanation, according to Wikipedia, is that "a round manhole cover cannot fall through its circular opening, whereas a square manhole cover may fall in if it were inserted diagonally in the hole."

2 Ron Suskind, "Amazon.com Debuts the Mother of All Bestseller Lists," *Washington Post,* August 26, 1998.

3 Ibid.

4 Jeff Bezos, speech to Commonwealth Club of California, July 27, 1998.

5 Jeff Bezos, speech to the American Association of Publishers, March 18, 1999.

6 Steven Levy, *In the Plex* (New York: Simon and Schuster, 2011), 34.

7 Jacqueline Doherty, "Amazon.bomb," *Barron's,* May 31, 1999.

8 George Anders, Nikhil Deogun, and Joann S. Lublin, "Joseph Galli Will Join Amazon, Reversing Plan to Take Pepsi Job," *Wall Street Journal,* June 25, 1999.

9 Joshua Cooper Ramo, "Jeff Bezos: King of the Internet," *Time,* December 27, 1999.

10 Stefanie Olsen, "FTC Fines E-Tailers $1.5 Million for Shipping Delays," CNET, July 26, 2000.

11 Michael Moe, "Tech Startup Secrets of Bill Campbell, Coach of Silicon Valley," *Forbes,* July 27, 2011.

Chapter 4: Milliravi

1 Jeremy Kahn, "The Giant Killer," *Fortune,* June 11, 2001.

2 Evelyn Nussenbaum, "Analyst Finally Tells Truth about Dot-Coms," *New York Post,* June 27, 2000.

3 Mark Leibovich, "Child Prodigy, Online Pioneer," *Washington Post,* September 3, 2000.

4 Ibid.

5 Steven Levy, "Jeff Bezos Owns the Web in More Ways Than You Think," *Wired,* November 13, 2011.

6 "Amazon.com Auctions Helps Online Sellers Become Effective Marketers," PR Newswire, August 18, 1999.

7 Scott Hillis, "Authors Protest Amazon's Practices, Used-Book Feature Comes under Fire," Reuters, December 28, 2000.

8 Jennifer Waters, "Amazon Faces 'Creditor Squeeze,'" *CBS MarketWatch,* February 6, 2001.

9 Gretchen Morgenson, "S.E.C. Is Said to Investigate Amazon Chief," *New York Times,* March 9, 2001.

10 Sinegal's comments are drawn from my July 2012 interview with Sinegal, the recollections of Amazon executives, and Andrew Bary, "King of the Jungle," *Barron's,* March 23, 2009.

11 Monica Soto, "Terrorist Attacks Overwhelm Amazon's Good News about Deal with Target," *Seattle Times,* September 27, 2001.

12 Saul Hansell, "Amazon Decides to Go for a Powerful Form of Advertising: Lower Prices and Word of Mouth," *New York Times,* February 10, 2003.

Part II
Chapter 5: Rocket Boy

1 Chip Bayers, "The Inner Bezos," *Wired,* March 1999.

2 Mark Leibovich, *The New Imperialists* (New York: Prentice Hall, 2002), 79.

3 "Local Team Wins Unicycle Polo Match," *Albuquerque Tribune,* November 23, 1961.

4 *Albuquerque Tribune,* April 24, 1965.

5 Leibovich, *The New Imperialists,* 73–74.

6 Ibid., 71.

7 Ibid., 74.

8 Jeff Bezos interview, Academy of Achievement, May 4, 2001.

9 "The World's Billionaires," *Forbes,* July 9, 2001.

10 Bayers, "The Inner Bezos."

11 Brad Stone, "Bezos in Space," *Newsweek,* May 5, 2003.

12 Mylene Mangalindan, "Buzz in West Texas Is about Bezos and His Launch Site," *Wall Street Journal,* November 10, 2006.

13 Jeff Bezos, "Successful Short Hop, Setback, and Next Vehicle," Blue Origin website, September 2, 2011.

14 Adam Lashinsky, "Amazon's Jeff Bezos: The Ultimate Disrupter," *Fortune,* November 16, 2012.

Chapter 6: Chaos Theory

1 Saul Hansell, "Listen Up! It's Time for a Profit; a Front-Row Seat as Amazon Gets Serious," *New York Times,* May 20, 2011.

2 Jeff Bezos, speech to the American Association of Publishers, March 18, 1999.

3 In 2012, my research assistant Nick Sanchez filed a comprehensive FOIA (Freedom of Information Act) request with the U.S. Department of Labor for any complaints or compliance violations for Amazon.com from 1995 through the present day. In addition to the much-publicized heat complaints reviewed by the *Allentown Morning Call,* regional and subregional OSHA offices returned a few

dozen employee complaints, including bathroom-break issues at a call center in Washington; forklift horseplay in New Hampshire; improper tornado sheltering in Pennsylvania; and concerns like water-cooler mineral buildup, breakroom mold, inadequate protective headgear, and harmful levels of noise and fumes. In all cases, Amazon responded to OSHA with evidence of compliance or immediately remedied the situation, and it settled the vast majority of concerns without need for OSHA inspection or citation. A $3,000 citation given to an Amazon Fresh center in Washington for not having an adequate emergency evacuation plan to deal with ammonia fumes was the most serious citation we found. But multijurisdiction FOIA requests have to be forwarded by the federal OSHA office to state and regional offices, and it is nearly impossible to obtain all such records for a company with a nationwide footprint as big as Amazon's, even with a year of lead time.

4 In July of 2012, Amazon established its Career Choice tuition-reimbursement program to help fulfillment-center employees with three consecutive years of service return to school to continue their education. Amazon said it would cover up to $2,000 a year in tuition for up to four years for each employee.

Chapter 7: A Technology Company, Not a Retailer

1 Gary Rivlin, "A Retail Revolution Turns Ten," *New York Times,* July 27, 2012.

2 Gary Wolf, "The Great Library of Amazonia," *Wired,* October 23, 2003.

3 Ibid.

4 Luke Timmerman, "Amazon's Top Techie, Werner Vogels, on How Web Services Follows the Retail Playbook," *Xconomy,* September 29, 2010.

5 Shobha Warrier, "From Studying under the Streetlights to CEO of a U.S. Firm!," *Rediff,* September 1, 2010.

6 Tim O'Reilly, "Amazon Web Services API," July 18, 2002, http://www.oreillynet.com/pub/wlg/1707.

7 Damien Cave, "Losing the War on Patents," *Salon,* February 15, 2002.

8 O'Reilly, "Amazon Web Services API."

9 Steve Grand, *Creation: Life and How to Make It* (Darby, PA: Diane Publishing, 2000), 132.

10 Hybrid machine/human computing arrangement patent filed October 12, 2001; http://www.google.com/patents/US7197459.

11 "Artificial Artificial Intelligence," *Economist,* June 10, 2006.

12 Katharine Mieszkowski, "I Make $1.45 a Week and I Love It," *Salon,* July 24, 2006.

13 Jason Pontin, "Artificial Intelligence, with Help from the Humans," *New York Times,* March 25, 2007.

14 Jeff Bezos, interview by Charlie Rose, *Charlie Rose,* PBS, February 26, 2009.

Chapter 8: Fiona

1 Calvin Reid, "Authors Guild Shoots Down Rocket eBook Contract," *Publishers Weekly,* May 10, 1999.

2 Steve Silberman, "Ex Libris," *Wired,* July 1998.

3 Steven Levy, "It's Time to Turn the Last Page," *Newsweek,* December 31, 1999.

4 Jane Spencer and Kara Scannell, "As Fraud Case Unravels, Executive Is at Large," *Wall Street Journal,* April 25, 2007.

5 David Pogue, "Trying Again to Make Books Obsolete," *New York Times,* October 12, 2006.

6 Jeff Bezos, speech at Lake Forest College, February 26, 1998.

7 Walt Mossberg, "The Way We Read," *Wall Street Journal,* June 9, 2008.

8 Mark Leibovich, "Child Prodigy, Online Pioneer," *Washington Post,* September 3, 2000.

9 Clayton Christensen, *The Innovator's Dilemma: When New Technologies Cause Great Firms to Fail* (Boston: Harvard Business Review Press, 1997).

10 Jeff Bezos, interview by Charlie Rose, *Charlie Rose,* PBS, February 26, 2009.

11 David D. Kirkpatrick, "Online Sales of Used Books Draw Protest," *New York Times,* April 10, 2002.

12 Graeme Neill, "Sony and Amazon in e-Books Battle," *Bookseller,* April 27, 2007.

13 Brad Stone, "Envisioning the Next Chapter for Electronic Books," *New York Times,* September 6, 2007.

14 Jeff Bezos, *The Oprah Winfrey Show,* ABC, October 24, 2008.

Part III:
Chapter 9: Liftoff!

1 Ben Charny, "Amazon Upgrade Leads Internet Stocks Higher," *MarketWatch,* January 22, 2007.

2 Victoria Barrett, "Too Smart for Its Own Good," *Forbes,* October 9, 2008.

3 Jim Collins, *Good to Great: Why Some Companies Make the Leap...and Others Don't* (New York: HarperCollins, 2001), 180.

Notes

4 Zappos Milestone: Timeline, Zappos.com, http://about.zappos.com/press-center/media-coverage/zappos-milestone-timeline.

5 Parija B. Kavilanz, "Circuit City to Shut Down," *CNN Money,* January 16, 2009.

6 Ben Austen, "The End of Borders and the Future of Books," *Bloomberg Businessweek,* November 10, 2011.

7 Annie Lowrey, "Readers Without Borders," *Slate,* July 20, 2011.

8 Scott Mayerowitz and Alice Gomstyn, "Target Among the Latest Chain of Grim Layoffs," ABC News, January 27, 2009.

9 Brad Stone, "Can Amazon Be the Wal-Mart of the Web?" *New York Times,* September 19, 2009.

10 Miguel Bustillo and Jeffrey A. Trachtenberg, "Wal-Mart Strafes Amazon in Book War," *Wall Street Journal,* October 16, 2009.

11 Brad Stone and Stephanie Rosenbloom, "Price War Brews Between Amazon and Wal-Mart," *New York Times,* November 23, 2009.

12 American Booksellers Association, Letter to Justice Department, October 22, 2009.

13 Spencer Wang, Credit Suisse First Boston analyst report, February 16, 2010.

14 Mick Rooney, "Amazon/Hachette Livre Dispute," *Independent Publishing Magazine,* June 6, 2008.

15 Eoin Purcell, "All Your Base Are Belong to Amazon," *Eoin Purcell's Blog,* May 14, 2009, http://eoinpurcellsblog.com/2009/05/14/all-your-base-are-belong-to-amazon/.

16 According to court testimony, on Jannuary 29, 2010, the general counsel of Simon & Schuster wrote to CEO Carolyn Kroll Reidy that she "cannot believe that Jobs made the statement" and considered it "incredibly stupid," http://www.nysd.uscourts.gov/cases/show.php?db=special&id=306, page 86.

17 Motoko Rich and Brad Stone, "Publisher Wins Fight with Amazon Over E-Books," *New York Times,* January 31, 2010.

Chapter 10: Expedient Convictions

1 Jeff Bezos, interview by Charlie Rose, *Charlie Rose,* PBS, July 28, 2010.

2 Fireside Chat with Jeff Bezos and Werner Vogels, Amazon Web Services re: Invent Conference, Las Vegas, November 29, 2012.

3 "Editorial: Spitzer's Latest Flop," *New York Sun,* November 15, 2007.

4 *Vadim Tsypin and Diana Tsypin v. Amazon.com et al.,* King County Superior Court, case 10-2-12192-7 SEA.

5 Miguel Bustillo and Stu Woo, "Retailers Push Amazon on Taxes," *Wall Street Journal,* March 17, 2011.

6 Aaron Glantz, "Amazon Spends Big to Fight Internet Sales Tax," *Bay Citizen,* August 27, 2011.

7 Tim O'Reilly, blog post, Google Plus, September 5, 2011, https://plus.google. com/+TimOReilly/posts/QypNDmvJJq7.

8 Zoe Corneli, "Legislature Approves Amazon Deal," *Bay Citizen,* September 9, 2011.

9 Bryant Urstadt, "What Amazon Fears Most: Diapers," *Bloomberg Businessweek,* October 7, 2010.

10 Nick Saint, "Amazon Nukes Diapers.com in Price War — May Force Diapers' Founders to Sell Out," *Business Insider,* November 5, 2010.

11 Amazon, "Amazon Marketplace Sellers Enjoy High-Growth Holiday Season," press release, January 2, 2013.

12 Roy Blount Jr., "The Kindle Swindle?," *New York Times,* February 24, 2009.

13 Brad Stone, "Amazon's Hit Man," *Bloomberg Businessweek,* January 25, 2012.

14 Thomas L. Friedman, "Do You Want the Good News First?," *New York Times,* May 19, 2012.

15 "Contracts on Fire: Amazon's Lending Library Mess," AuthorsGuild.org, November 14, 2011.

16 Richard Russo, "Amazon's Jungle Logic," *New York Times,* December 12, 2011.

Chapter 11: The Kingdom of the Question Mark

1 George Anders, "Inside Amazon's Idea Machine: How Bezos Decodes the Customer," *Forbes,* April 4, 2012.

2 Amazon's Leadership Principles, http://www.amazon.com/Values-Careers-Homepage/b?ie=UTF8&node=239365011.

3 Luisa Kroll and Kerry A. Dolan, "The World's Billionaires," *Forbes,* March 4, 2013.

4 David Dykstra, "Bezos Completes $28 Million Home Improvement," Seattle-Mansions.Blogspot.com, October 1, 2010, http://seattle-mansions.blogspot. com/2010/10/bezos-completes-28-million-home.html.

5 Rebecca Johnson, "MacKenzie Bezos: Writer, Mother of Four, and High-Profile Wife," *Vogue,* February 20, 2013.

Index

Index

Index

Index

Index

Index

Index

Index

Index

Index

About the Author

Brad Stone has covered Amazon and technology in Silicon Valley for fifteen years for publications such as *Newsweek* and the *New York Times*. He is currently a senior writer for *Bloomberg Business-week* and lives in San Francisco, California. Visit him online at www.brad-stone.com.